TEACHER'S PET PUBLICATIONS

PUZZLE PACK
for
Flowers For Algernon

based on the book by
Daniel Keyes

Written by
William T. Collins

© 2005 Teacher's Pet Publications
All Rights Reserved

The materials in this packet are copyrighted
by Teacher's Pet Publications, Inc.

These pages may be duplicated by the purchaser
for use in the purchaser's own classroom.

Copying any of these materials and distributing them
for any other purpose is a violation of the copyright laws.

© 2005 Teacher's Pet Publications, Inc.
www.tpet.com

INTRODUCTION
If you already own the LitPlan for this title, this Puzzle Pack will refresh your Unit Resource Materials and Vocabulary Resource Materials sections plus give you additional materials you can substitute into the tests. If you do not already have a complete LitPlan, these pages will give you some supplemental materials to use with your own plan. There are two main groups of materials: one set for unit words (such as characters' names, symbols, places, etc.) and one set for vocabulary words associated with the book.

WORD LIST
There is a word list for both the unit words and the vocabulary words. These lists show you which words are being used in the materials and the clues or definitions being used for those words. You may want to give students a word list with clues/definitions to help them, or you may want students to only have a word list (without clues/definitions) if you want them to work a little harder. Both are available for duplication. The word lists can also be your "calling key" for the bingo games.

FILL IN THE BLANK AND MATCHING
There are 4 each of the fill in the blank and matching worksheets for both the unit and vocabulary words. These pages can be used either as extra worksheets for students or as objective parts of a unit test. They can be done individually if students need extra help or as a whole class activity to review the material covered.

MAGIC SQUARES
The magic squares not only reinforce the material covered but also work on reasoning and math skills. Many teachers have told us that their students really enjoy doing these!

WORD SEARCH PUZZLES
The word search words go in all directions, as indicated on your answer keys. Two of the word search puzzles have the clues listed rather than the words. This makes the puzzle a little more difficult, but it reinforces the material better. Two word search puzzles have words only for students who find the clue puzzles too difficult.

CROSSWORD PUZZLES
Both unit and vocabulary word sections have 4 crossword puzzles.

BINGO CARDS
There are 32 individual bingo cards for the unit words and 32 individual bingo cards for the vocabulary words. You can use your word list as a "call list," calling the words at random and marking them off of your list as you go, or you could use the flash cards by cutting them apart and drawing the words at random from a hat (or box or whatever). To make a better review, you might ask for the definition and spelling of each word as you call it out–or you could call out the definitions and have students tell you the words they need to look for on the puzzle.

JUGGLE LETTERS
The vocabulary juggle letter game is intended to help students learn the spellings of the words. One sheet has the definitions listed on it as an extra help for students who need it or to reinforce the definitions if you choose to do so.

FLASH CARDS
We've included a set of vocabulary flash cards you can duplicate, cut, and fold for your students. Some teachers make a few sets for general use by the class; others make a set for each student. Some teachers duplicate them for each student and have the students cut & fold their own. You can cut out just the words and put them in a hat, have each student pick out one word and write the definition and a sentence for that word. Students then swap words and papers, with the next student adding a sentence of his own under the last one. You can have students swap as many times as you like. Each time the student will read the sentences written prior to his own and then add a sentence. You can cut out the words and definitions separately and play "I Have; Who Has?" Each student in the room draws a word and definition. The first student says, "I have (the name of the word). Who has the definition?" The student with the definition reads it then says, "I have (the name of the vocabulary word she has). Who has the definition?" The round continues until all words and definitions have been given.

Flowers For Algernon Unit Word List

No.	Word	Clue/Definition
1.	ALGERNON	Mouse with increased intelligence
2.	ALICE	Teacher with whom Charlie fell in love
3.	BAKERY	Where Charlie worked
4.	BARBER	Shop Matt wanted to own
5.	BEEKMAN	College for Retarded Adults
6.	CHARLIE	Wanted to be smart to have people like him
7.	DANCING	Charlie's pastime with Fay
8.	DETERIORATED	What happened to artificially increased intelligence
9.	DIED	What happened to Algernon
10.	DONNER	Owner of bakery
11.	DREAMS	Charlie found them disturbing
12.	DRUNK	Charlie's condition at Mrs. Nemur's party
13.	ESCAPE	Charlie and Agernon did this in Chicago
14.	FRANK	He said he was as good as Charlie
15.	GIMPY	Stole from Mr. Donner
16.	GORDON	Charlie's family name
17.	GRAVE	Where Charlie wanted flowers for Algernon
18.	GUARINO	Dr. who treated Charlie like a human being
19.	IQ	Charlie's increased
20.	KEYES	Author
21.	KINNIAN	Alice's last name
22.	LABORATORY	Where experiments were done
23.	LILLMAN	Fay who was full of life and excitement
24.	LOVE	Charlie's feeling for Alice
25.	MATT	Charlie's father
26.	MAZE	Algernon and Charlie competed at this
27.	MEMORIES	They gradually returned to Charlie
28.	NEMUR	An ordinary man trying to do a great man's work
29.	NORMA	Charlie's sister
30.	NOVEMBER	Date of last progress report; ___ 21st
31.	OPERATION	How Charlie's intelligence increased
32.	PROGRESS	March 3 was the date of the first ___ report
33.	REPORT	Vehicle for telling the story; progress ___
34.	RORSCHACH	Inkblot test
35.	ROSE	Charlie's mother
36.	SELDEN	Administered inkblot and other tests
37.	SMART	What Charlie wanted to be
38.	STRAUSS	Psychiatrist and neurosurgeon
39.	TEACHER	Alice Kinnian's occupation
40.	WARREN	State Home and Training School
41.	WELBERG	Foundation that provided money for experiment

Copyrighted

Flowers for Algernon Fill In The Blank 1

_____ 1. Stole from Mr. Donner

_____ 2. Mouse with increased intelligence

_____ 3. Date of last progress report; ___ 21st

_____ 4. How Charlie's intelligence increased

_____ 5. Where experiments were done

_____ 6. Charlie's pastime with Fay

_____ 7. Charlie's father

_____ 8. He said he was as good as Charlie

_____ 9. What happened to artificially increased intelligence

_____ 10. Foundation that provided money for experiment

_____ 11. Charlie's increased

_____ 12. Dr. who treated Charlie like a human being

_____ 13. Where Charlie worked

_____ 14. Charlie's feeling for Alice

_____ 15. They gradually returned to Charlie

_____ 16. Charlie's family name

_____ 17. Wanted to be smart to have people like him

_____ 18. Charlie found them disturbing

_____ 19. Algernon and Charlie competed at this

_____ 20. Where Charlie wanted flowers for Algernon

Flowers for Algernon Fill In The Blank 1 Answer Key

GIMPY	1. Stole from Mr. Donner
ALGERNON	2. Mouse with increased intelligence
NOVEMBER	3. Date of last progress report; ___ 21st
OPERATION	4. How Charlie's intelligence increased
LABORATORY	5. Where experiments were done
DANCING	6. Charlie's pastime with Fay
MATT	7. Charlie's father
FRANK	8. He said he was as good as Charlie
DETERIORATED	9. What happened to artificially increased intelligence
WELBERG	10. Foundation that provided money for experiment
IQ	11. Charlie's increased
GUARINO	12. Dr. who treated Charlie like a human being
BAKERY	13. Where Charlie worked
LOVE	14. Charlie's feeling for Alice
MEMORIES	15. They gradually returned to Charlie
GORDON	16. Charlie's family name
CHARLIE	17. Wanted to be smart to have people like him
DREAMS	18. Charlie found them disturbing
MAZE	19. Algernon and Charlie competed at this
GRAVE	20. Where Charlie wanted flowers for Algernon

Flowers for Algernon Fill In The Blank 2

_____ 1. Inkblot test

_____ 2. Charlie's feeling for Alice

_____ 3. Charlie found them disturbing

_____ 4. Vehicle for telling the story; progress ___

_____ 5. What happened to Algernon

_____ 6. Dr. who treated Charlie like a human being

_____ 7. What Charlie wanted to be

_____ 8. Author

_____ 9. Where Charlie worked

_____ 10. Where Charlie wanted flowers for Algernon

_____ 11. He said he was as good as Charlie

_____ 12. March 3 was the date of the first ___ report

_____ 13. Charlie's mother

_____ 14. Owner of bakery

_____ 15. An ordinary man trying to do a great man's work

_____ 16. State Home and Training School

_____ 17. Date of last progress report; ___ 21st

_____ 18. Teacher with whom Charlie fell in love

_____ 19. Charlie and Agernon did this in Chicago

_____ 20. Charlie's condition at Mrs. Nemur's party

Flowers for Algernon Fill In The Blank 2 Answer Key

RORSCHACH	1. Inkblot test
LOVE	2. Charlie's feeling for Alice
DREAMS	3. Charlie found them disturbing
REPORT	4. Vehicle for telling the story; progress ___
DIED	5. What happened to Algernon
GUARINO	6. Dr. who treated Charlie like a human being
SMART	7. What Charlie wanted to be
KEYES	8. Author
BAKERY	9. Where Charlie worked
GRAVE	10. Where Charlie wanted flowers for Algernon
FRANK	11. He said he was as good as Charlie
PROGRESS	12. March 3 was the date of the first ___ report
ROSE	13. Charlie's mother
DONNER	14. Owner of bakery
NEMUR	15. An ordinary man trying to do a great man's work
WARREN	16. State Home and Training School
NOVEMBER	17. Date of last progress report; ___ 21st
ALICE	18. Teacher with whom Charlie fell in love
ESCAPE	19. Charlie and Agernon did this in Chicago
DRUNK	20. Charlie's condition at Mrs. Nemur's party

Flowers for Algernon Fill In The Blank 3

_____ 1. Where Charlie wanted flowers for Algernon
_____ 2. He said he was as good as Charlie
_____ 3. Charlie and Agernon did this in Chicago
_____ 4. Administered inkblot and other tests
_____ 5. Dr. who treated Charlie like a human being
_____ 6. Fay who was full of life and excitement
_____ 7. An ordinary man trying to do a great man's work
_____ 8. What happened to Algernon
_____ 9. Charlie's pastime with Fay
_____ 10. Charlie's mother
_____ 11. Algernon and Charlie competed at this
_____ 12. How Charlie's intelligence increased
_____ 13. Charlie's condition at Mrs. Nemur's party
_____ 14. Mouse with increased intelligence
_____ 15. Psychiatrist and neurosurgeon
_____ 16. Teacher with whom Charlie fell in love
_____ 17. Date of last progress report; ___ 21st
_____ 18. Wanted to be smart to have people like him
_____ 19. Charlie's father
_____ 20. What Charlie wanted to be

Flowers for Algernon Fill In The Blank 3 Answer Key

GRAVE	1. Where Charlie wanted flowers for Algernon
FRANK	2. He said he was as good as Charlie
ESCAPE	3. Charlie and Agernon did this in Chicago
SELDEN	4. Administered inkblot and other tests
GUARINO	5. Dr. who treated Charlie like a human being
LILLMAN	6. Fay who was full of life and excitement
NEMUR	7. An ordinary man trying to do a great man's work
DIED	8. What happened to Algernon
DANCING	9. Charlie's pastime with Fay
ROSE	10. Charlie's mother
MAZE	11. Algernon and Charlie competed at this
OPERATION	12. How Charlie's intelligence increased
DRUNK	13. Charlie's condition at Mrs. Nemur's party
ALGERNON	14. Mouse with increased intelligence
STRAUSS	15. Psychiatrist and neurosurgeon
ALICE	16. Teacher with whom Charlie fell in love
NOVEMBER	17. Date of last progress report; ___ 21st
CHARLIE	18. Wanted to be smart to have people like him
MATT	19. Charlie's father
SMART	20. What Charlie wanted to be

Copyrighted

Flowers for Algernon Fill In The Blank 4

_____ 1. Charlie's family name

_____ 2. Owner of bakery

_____ 3. Charlie and Agernon did this in Chicago

_____ 4. Administered inkblot and other tests

_____ 5. They gradually returned to Charlie

_____ 6. Shop Matt wanted to own

_____ 7. Wanted to be smart to have people like him

_____ 8. How Charlie's intelligence increased

_____ 9. Alice's last name

_____ 10. He said he was as good as Charlie

_____ 11. Charlie's increased

_____ 12. Vehicle for telling the story; progress ___

_____ 13. Stole from Mr. Donner

_____ 14. An ordinary man trying to do a great man's work

_____ 15. Mouse with increased intelligence

_____ 16. What happened to Algernon

_____ 17. Where Charlie wanted flowers for Algernon

_____ 18. Fay who was full of life and excitement

_____ 19. Charlie's pastime with Fay

_____ 20. Charlie's feeling for Alice

Flowers for Algernon Fill In The Blank 4 Answer key

GORDON	1. Charlie's family name
DONNER	2. Owner of bakery
ESCAPE	3. Charlie and Agernon did this in Chicago
SELDEN	4. Administered inkblot and other tests
MEMORIES	5. They gradually returned to Charlie
BARBER	6. Shop Matt wanted to own
CHARLIE	7. Wanted to be smart to have people like him
OPERATION	8. How Charlie's intelligence increased
KINNIAN	9. Alice's last name
FRANK	10. He said he was as good as Charlie
IQ	11. Charlie's increased
REPORT	12. Vehicle for telling the story; progress ___
GIMPY	13. Stole from Mr. Donner
NEMUR	14. An ordinary man trying to do a great man's work
ALGERNON	15. Mouse with increased intelligence
DIED	16. What happened to Algernon
GRAVE	17. Where Charlie wanted flowers for Algernon
LILLMAN	18. Fay who was full of life and excitement
DANCING	19. Charlie's pastime with Fay
LOVE	20. Charlie's feeling for Alice

Flowers for Algernon Matching 1

___ 1. IQ
___ 2. ALGERNON
___ 3. MAZE
___ 4. BAKERY
___ 5. DETERIORATED
___ 6. DANCING
___ 7. DIED
___ 8. ROSE
___ 9. RORSCHACH
___ 10. GRAVE
___ 11. OPERATION
___ 12. BARBER
___ 13. MATT
___ 14. LABORATORY
___ 15. NOVEMBER
___ 16. NORMA
___ 17. STRAUSS
___ 18. KEYES
___ 19. ESCAPE
___ 20. PROGRESS
___ 21. DONNER
___ 22. KINNIAN
___ 23. NEMUR
___ 24. CHARLIE
___ 25. GUARINO

A. Charlie's mother
B. Charlie's increased
C. March 3 was the date of the first ___ report
D. Inkblot test
E. Alice's last name
F. Where Charlie wanted flowers for Algernon
G. What happened to artificially increased intelligence
H. Where Charlie worked
I. Owner of bakery
J. Mouse with increased intelligence
K. Charlie and Agernon did this in Chicago
L. Date of last progress report; ___ 21st
M. Charlie's father
N. Algernon and Charlie competed at this
O. Dr. who treated Charlie like a human being
P. An ordinary man trying to do a great man's work
Q. Where experiments were done
R. What happened to Algernon
S. Charlie's pastime with Fay
T. Charlie's sister
U. Psychiatrist and neurosurgeon
V. Shop Matt wanted to own
W. Author
X. How Charlie's intelligence increased
Y. Wanted to be smart to have people like him

Flowers for Algernon Matching 1 Answer Key

B - 1. IQ		A. Charlie's mother
J - 2. ALGERNON		B. Charlie's increased
N - 3. MAZE		C. March 3 was the date of the first ___ report
H - 4. BAKERY		D. Inkblot test
G - 5. DETERIORATED		E. Alice's last name
S - 6. DANCING		F. Where Charlie wanted flowers for Algernon
R - 7. DIED		G. What happened to artificially increased intelligence
A - 8. ROSE		H. Where Charlie worked
D - 9. RORSCHACH		I. Owner of bakery
F - 10. GRAVE		J. Mouse with increased intelligence
X - 11. OPERATION		K. Charlie and Agernon did this in Chicago
V - 12. BARBER		L. Date of last progress report; ___ 21st
M - 13. MATT		M. Charlie's father
Q - 14. LABORATORY		N. Algernon and Charlie competed at this
L - 15. NOVEMBER		O. Dr. who treated Charlie like a human being
T - 16. NORMA		P. An ordinary man trying to do a great man's work
U - 17. STRAUSS		Q. Where experiments were done
W - 18. KEYES		R. What happened to Algernon
K - 19. ESCAPE		S. Charlie's pastime with Fay
C - 20. PROGRESS		T. Charlie's sister
I - 21. DONNER		U. Psychiatrist and neurosurgeon
E - 22. KINNIAN		V. Shop Matt wanted to own
P - 23. NEMUR		W. Author
Y - 24. CHARLIE		X. How Charlie's intelligence increased
O - 25. GUARINO		Y. Wanted to be smart to have people like him

Copyrighted

Flowers for Algernon Matching 2

___ 1. ROSE   A. An ordinary man trying to do a great man's work
___ 2. MATT   B. Where experiments were done
___ 3. ALICE   C. State Home and Training School
___ 4. WARREN   D. Alice Kinnian's occupation
___ 5. DETERIORATED   E. Charlie's condition at Mrs. Nemur's party
___ 6. CHARLIE   F. March 3 was the date of the first ___ report
___ 7. IQ   G. Fay who was full of life and excitement
___ 8. WELBERG   H. Date of last progress report; ___ 21st
___ 9. TEACHER   I. Charlie's mother
___10. STRAUSS   J. Foundation that provided money for experiment
___11. LILLMAN   K. Charlie's feeling for Alice
___12. PROGRESS   L. Where Charlie wanted flowers for Algernon
___13. RORSCHACH   M. What happened to artificially increased intelligence
___14. LOVE   N. Author
___15. DREAMS   O. Psychiatrist and neurosurgeon
___16. DRUNK   P. Where Charlie worked
___17. KEYES   Q. They gradually returned to Charlie
___18. MEMORIES   R. Charlie's father
___19. NEMUR   S. Wanted to be smart to have people like him
___20. BAKERY   T. Charlie's increased
___21. LABORATORY   U. Teacher with whom Charlie fell in love
___22. GRAVE   V. Inkblot test
___23. REPORT   W. Alice's last name
___24. KINNIAN   X. Charlie found them disturbing
___25. NOVEMBER   Y. Vehicle for telling the story; progress ___

Flowers for Algernon Matching 2 Answer Key

I -	1. ROSE	A.	An ordinary man trying to do a great man's work
R -	2. MATT	B.	Where experiments were done
U -	3. ALICE	C.	State Home and Training School
C -	4. WARREN	D.	Alice Kinnian's occupation
M -	5. DETERIORATED	E.	Charlie's condition at Mrs. Nemur's party
S -	6. CHARLIE	F.	March 3 was the date of the first ___ report
T -	7. IQ	G.	Fay who was full of life and excitement
J -	8. WELBERG	H.	Date of last progress report; ___ 21st
D -	9. TEACHER	I.	Charlie's mother
O -	10. STRAUSS	J.	Foundation that provided money for experiment
G -	11. LILLMAN	K.	Charlie's feeling for Alice
F -	12. PROGRESS	L.	Where Charlie wanted flowers for Algernon
V -	13. RORSCHACH	M.	What happened to artificially increased intelligence
K -	14. LOVE	N.	Author
X -	15. DREAMS	O.	Psychiatrist and neurosurgeon
E -	16. DRUNK	P.	Where Charlie worked
N -	17. KEYES	Q.	They gradually returned to Charlie
Q -	18. MEMORIES	R.	Charlie's father
A -	19. NEMUR	S.	Wanted to be smart to have people like him
P -	20. BAKERY	T.	Charlie's increased
B -	21. LABORATORY	U.	Teacher with whom Charlie fell in love
L -	22. GRAVE	V.	Inkblot test
Y -	23. REPORT	W.	Alice's last name
W -	24. KINNIAN	X.	Charlie found them disturbing
H -	25. NOVEMBER	Y.	Vehicle for telling the story; progress ___

Copyrighted

Flowers for Algernon Matching 3

___ 1. LABORATORY   A. Where Charlie worked
___ 2. WARREN   B. What Charlie wanted to be
___ 3. LOVE   C. Date of last progress report; ___ 21st
___ 4. CHARLIE   D. Administered inkblot and other tests
___ 5. PROGRESS   E. Charlie's father
___ 6. ALGERNON   F. College for Retarded Adults
___ 7. WELBERG   G. Dr. who treated Charlie like a human being
___ 8. GIMPY   H. March 3 was the date of the first ___ report
___ 9. RORSCHACH   I. Wanted to be smart to have people like him
___ 10. NEMUR   J. Charlie's feeling for Alice
___ 11. SMART   K. Inkblot test
___ 12. BAKERY   L. An ordinary man trying to do a great man's work
___ 13. NOVEMBER   M. Algernon and Charlie competed at this
___ 14. IQ   N. They gradually returned to Charlie
___ 15. GUARINO   O. Where experiments were done
___ 16. BEEKMAN   P. Alice's last name
___ 17. MAZE   Q. Stole from Mr. Donner
___ 18. MEMORIES   R. Charlie found them disturbing
___ 19. FRANK   S. Foundation that provided money for experiment
___ 20. KINNIAN   T. Charlie's increased
___ 21. MATT   U. He said he was as good as Charlie
___ 22. ROSE   V. Charlie's mother
___ 23. SELDEN   W. Mouse with increased intelligence
___ 24. DREAMS   X. State Home and Training School
___ 25. LILLMAN   Y. Fay who was full of life and excitement

Flowers for Algernon Matching 3 Answer Key

O - 1. LABORATORY	A.	Where Charlie worked
X - 2. WARREN	B.	What Charlie wanted to be
J - 3. LOVE	C.	Date of last progress report; ___ 21st
I - 4. CHARLIE	D.	Administered inkblot and other tests
H - 5. PROGRESS	E.	Charlie's father
W - 6. ALGERNON	F.	College for Retarded Adults
S - 7. WELBERG	G.	Dr. who treated Charlie like a human being
Q - 8. GIMPY	H.	March 3 was the date of the first ___ report
K - 9. RORSCHACH	I.	Wanted to be smart to have people like him
L - 10. NEMUR	J.	Charlie's feeling for Alice
B - 11. SMART	K.	Inkblot test
A - 12. BAKERY	L.	An ordinary man trying to do a great man's work
C - 13. NOVEMBER	M.	Algernon and Charlie competed at this
T - 14. IQ	N.	They gradually returned to Charlie
G - 15. GUARINO	O.	Where experiments were done
F - 16. BEEKMAN	P.	Alice's last name
M - 17. MAZE	Q.	Stole from Mr. Donner
N - 18. MEMORIES	R.	Charlie found them disturbing
U - 19. FRANK	S.	Foundation that provided money for experiment
P - 20. KINNIAN	T.	Charlie's increased
E - 21. MATT	U.	He said he was as good as Charlie
V - 22. ROSE	V.	Charlie's mother
D - 23. SELDEN	W.	Mouse with increased intelligence
R - 24. DREAMS	X.	State Home and Training School
Y - 25. LILLMAN	Y.	Fay who was full of life and excitement

Flowers for Algernon Matching 4

___ 1. TEACHER   A. Charlie's father
___ 2. ALICE   B. Date of last progress report; ___ 21st
___ 3. NOVEMBER   C. What happened to Algernon
___ 4. BARBER   D. An ordinary man trying to do a great man's work
___ 5. CHARLIE   E. Charlie's family name
___ 6. PROGRESS   F. College for Retarded Adults
___ 7. GRAVE   G. Fay who was full of life and excitement
___ 8. NEMUR   H. Owner of bakery
___ 9. REPORT   I. Administered inkblot and other tests
___ 10. OPERATION   J. Where Charlie wanted flowers for Algernon
___ 11. MATT   K. Alice Kinnian's occupation
___ 12. GIMPY   L. Vehicle for telling the story; progress ___
___ 13. LILLMAN   M. Alice's last name
___ 14. STRAUSS   N. Foundation that provided money for experiment
___ 15. KINNIAN   O. Stole from Mr. Donner
___ 16. BEEKMAN   P. They gradually returned to Charlie
___ 17. SELDEN   Q. How Charlie's intelligence increased
___ 18. MEMORIES   R. Psychiatrist and neurosurgeon
___ 19. GORDON   S. Shop Matt wanted to own
___ 20. DONNER   T. Charlie found them disturbing
___ 21. IQ   U. Wanted to be smart to have people like him
___ 22. DRUNK   V. Charlie's condition at Mrs. Nemur's party
___ 23. DREAMS   W. March 3 was the date of the first ___ report
___ 24. WELBERG   X. Charlie's increased
___ 25. DIED   Y. Teacher with whom Charlie fell in love

Flowers for Algernon Matching 4 Answer Key

K - 1.	TEACHER	A.	Charlie's father
Y - 2.	ALICE	B.	Date of last progress report; ___ 21st
B - 3.	NOVEMBER	C.	What happened to Algernon
S - 4.	BARBER	D.	An ordinary man trying to do a great man's work
U - 5.	CHARLIE	E.	Charlie's family name
W - 6.	PROGRESS	F.	College for Retarded Adults
J - 7.	GRAVE	G.	Fay who was full of life and excitement
D - 8.	NEMUR	H.	Owner of bakery
L - 9.	REPORT	I.	Administered inkblot and other tests
Q -10.	OPERATION	J.	Where Charlie wanted flowers for Algernon
A -11.	MATT	K.	Alice Kinnian's occupation
O -12.	GIMPY	L.	Vehicle for telling the story; progress ___
G -13.	LILLMAN	M.	Alice's last name
R -14.	STRAUSS	N.	Foundation that provided money for experiment
M -15.	KINNIAN	O.	Stole from Mr. Donner
F -16.	BEEKMAN	P.	They gradually returned to Charlie
I -17.	SELDEN	Q.	How Charlie's intelligence increased
P -18.	MEMORIES	R.	Psychiatrist and neurosurgeon
E -19.	GORDON	S.	Shop Matt wanted to own
H -20.	DONNER	T.	Charlie found them disturbing
X -21.	IQ	U.	Wanted to be smart to have people like him
V -22.	DRUNK	V.	Charlie's condition at Mrs. Nemur's party
T -23.	DREAMS	W.	March 3 was the date of the first ___ report
N -24.	WELBERG	X.	Charlie's increased
C -25.	DIED	Y.	Teacher with whom Charlie fell in love

Flowers for Algernon Magic Squares 1

Match the definition with the vocabulary word. Put your answers in the magic squares below. When your answers are correct, all columns and rows will add to the same number.

A. GRAVE   E. GUARINO   I. BARBER   M. REPORT
B. BAKERY   F. STRAUSS   J. DETERIORATED   N. MAZE
C. SMART   G. ESCAPE   K. KINNIAN   O. GIMPY
D. ALGERNON   H. ROSE   L. MEMORIES   P. ALICE

1. Psychiatrist and neurosurgeon
2. Shop Matt wanted to own
3. Stole from Mr. Donner
4. Mouse with increased intelligence
5. Vehicle for telling the story; progress ___
6. Where Charlie worked
7. Charlie's mother
8. Alice's last name
9. What Charlie wanted to be
10. Teacher with whom Charlie fell in love
11. What happened to artificially increased intelligence
12. Dr. who treated Charlie like a human being
13. They gradually returned to Charlie
14. Charlie and Agernon did this in Chicago
15. Where Charlie wanted flowers for Algernon
16. Algernon and Charlie competed at this

A=	B=	C=	D=
E=	F=	G=	H=
I=	J=	K=	L=
M=	N=	O=	P=

Flowers for Algernon Magic Squares 1 Answer Key

Match the definition with the vocabulary word. Put your answers in the magic squares below. When your answers are correct, all columns and rows will add to the same number.

A. GRAVE
B. BAKERY
C. SMART
D. ALGERNON
E. GUARINO
F. STRAUSS
G. ESCAPE
H. ROSE
I. BARBER
J. DETERIORATED
K. KINNIAN
L. MEMORIES
M. REPORT
N. MAZE
O. GIMPY
P. ALICE

1. Psychiatrist and neurosurgeon
2. Shop Matt wanted to own
3. Stole from Mr. Donner
4. Mouse with increased intelligence
5. Vehicle for telling the story; progress ___
6. Where Charlie worked
7. Charlie's mother
8. Alice's last name
9. What Charlie wanted to be
10. Teacher with whom Charlie fell in love
11. What happened to artificially increased intelligence
12. Dr. who treated Charlie like a human being
13. They gradually returned to Charlie
14. Charlie and Agernon did this in Chicago
15. Where Charlie wanted flowers for Algernon
16. Algernon and Charlie competed at this

A=15	B=6	C=9	D=4
E=12	F=1	G=14	H=7
I=2	J=11	K=8	L=13
M=5	N=16	O=3	P=10

Flowers for Algernon Magic Squares 2

Match the definition with the vocabulary word. Put your answers in the magic squares below. When your answers are correct, all columns and rows will add to the same number.

A. NOVEMBER
B. ALICE
C. FRANK
D. REPORT
E. SMART
F. CHARLIE
G. ALGERNON
H. DONNER
I. KEYES
J. BARBER
K. GORDON
L. MEMORIES
M. BAKERY
N. GRAVE
O. WARREN
P. LABORATORY

1. Where Charlie worked
2. Wanted to be smart to have people like him
3. Owner of bakery
4. State Home and Training School
5. They gradually returned to Charlie
6. He said he was as good as Charlie
7. Date of last progress report; ___ 21st
8. Shop Matt wanted to own
9. Charlie's family name
10. Vehicle for telling the story; progress ___
11. Teacher with whom Charlie fell in love
12. Author
13. Where Charlie wanted flowers for Algernon
14. What Charlie wanted to be
15. Mouse with increased intelligence
16. Where experiments were done

A=	B=	C=	D=
E=	F=	G=	H=
I=	J=	K=	L=
M=	N=	O=	P=

Flowers for Algernon Magic Squares 2 Answer Key

Match the definition with the vocabulary word. Put your answers in the magic squares below. When your answers are correct, all columns and rows will add to the same number.

A. NOVEMBER   E. SMART   I. KEYES   M. BAKERY
B. ALICE   F. CHARLIE   J. BARBER   N. GRAVE
C. FRANK   G. ALGERNON   K. GORDON   O. WARREN
D. REPORT   H. DONNER   L. MEMORIES   P. LABORATORY

1. Where Charlie worked
2. Wanted to be smart to have people like him
3. Owner of bakery
4. State Home and Training School
5. They gradually returned to Charlie
6. He said he was as good as Charlie
7. Date of last progress report; ___ 21st
8. Shop Matt wanted to own
9. Charlie's family name
10. Vehicle for telling the story; progress ___
11. Teacher with whom Charlie fell in love
12. Author
13. Where Charlie wanted flowers for Algernon
14. What Charlie wanted to be
15. Mouse with increased intelligence
16. Where experiments were done

A=7	B=11	C=6	D=10
E=14	F=2	G=15	H=3
I=12	J=8	K=9	L=5
M=1	N=13	O=4	P=16

Flowers for Algernon Magic Squares 3

Match the definition with the vocabulary word. Put your answers in the magic squares below. When your answers are correct, all columns and rows will add to the same number.

A. DREAMS
B. SELDEN
C. ALGERNON
D. BARBER
E. SMART
F. MATT
G. MAZE
H. FRANK
I. REPORT
J. LABORATORY
K. DONNER
L. RORSCHACH
M. GUARINO
N. DRUNK
O. KEYES
P. GIMPY

1. Charlie found them disturbing
2. Charlie's condition at Mrs. Nemur's party
3. Where experiments were done
4. What Charlie wanted to be
5. Algernon and Charlie competed at this
6. Inkblot test
7. Stole from Mr. Donner
8. Mouse with increased intelligence
9. Author
10. Shop Matt wanted to own
11. He said he was as good as Charlie
12. Owner of bakery
13. Vehicle for telling the story; progress ___
14. Charlie's father
15. Administered inkblot and other tests
16. Dr. who treated Charlie like a human being

A=	B=	C=	D=
E=	F=	G=	H=
I=	J=	K=	L=
M=	N=	O=	P=

Flowers for Algernon Magic Squares 3 Answer Key

Match the definition with the vocabulary word. Put your answers in the magic squares below. When your answers are correct, all columns and rows will add to the same number.

A. DREAMS
B. SELDEN
C. ALGERNON
D. BARBER
E. SMART
F. MATT
G. MAZE
H. FRANK
I. REPORT
J. LABORATORY
K. DONNER
L. RORSCHACH
M. GUARINO
N. DRUNK
O. KEYES
P. GIMPY

1. Charlie found them disturbing
2. Charlie's condition at Mrs. Nemur's party
3. Where experiments were done
4. What Charlie wanted to be
5. Algernon and Charlie competed at this
6. Inkblot test
7. Stole from Mr. Donner
8. Mouse with increased intelligence
9. Author
10. Shop Matt wanted to own
11. He said he was as good as Charlie
12. Owner of bakery
13. Vehicle for telling the story; progress ___
14. Charlie's father
15. Administered inkblot and other tests
16. Dr. who treated Charlie like a human being

A=1	B=15	C=8	D=10
E=4	F=14	G=5	H=11
I=13	J=3	K=12	L=6
M=16	N=2	O=9	P=7

Flowers for Algernon Magic Squares 4

Match the definition with the vocabulary word. Put your answers in the magic squares below. When your answers are correct, all columns and rows will add to the same number.

A. ESCAPE
B. GUARINO
C. KINNIAN
D. SELDEN
E. MEMORIES
F. NORMA
G. ROSE
H. BAKERY
I. ALICE
J. OPERATION
K. RORSCHACH
L. NOVEMBER
M. NEMUR
N. MAZE
O. DIED
P. MATT

1. What happened to Algernon
2. How Charlie's intelligence increased
3. Where Charlie worked
4. Charlie and Agernon did this in Chicago
5. Administered inkblot and other tests
6. They gradually returned to Charlie
7. Inkblot test
8. Algernon and Charlie competed at this
9. Charlie's sister
10. Alice's last name
11. An ordinary man trying to do a great man's work
12. Date of last progress report; ___ 21st
13. Teacher with whom Charlie fell in love
14. Charlie's father
15. Dr. who treated Charlie like a human being
16. Charlie's mother

A=	B=	C=	D=
E=	F=	G=	H=
I=	J=	K=	L=
M=	N=	O=	P=

Flowers for Algernon Magic Squares 4 Answer Key

Match the definition with the vocabulary word. Put your answers in the magic squares below. When your answers are correct, all columns and rows will add to the same number.

A. ESCAPE   E. MEMORIES   I. ALICE   M. NEMUR
B. GUARINO   F. NORMA   J. OPERATION   N. MAZE
C. KINNIAN   G. ROSE   K. RORSCHACH   O. DIED
D. SELDEN   H. BAKERY   L. NOVEMBER   P. MATT

1. What happened to Algernon
2. How Charlie's intelligence increased
3. Where Charlie worked
4. Charlie and Agernon did this in Chicago
5. Administered inkblot and other tests
6. They gradually returned to Charlie
7. Inkblot test
8. Algernon and Charlie competed at this
9. Charlie's sister
10. Alice's last name
11. An ordinary man trying to do a great man's work
12. Date of last progress report; ___ 21st
13. Teacher with whom Charlie fell in love
14. Charlie's father
15. Dr. who treated Charlie like a human being
16. Charlie's mother

A=4	B=15	C=10	D=5
E=6	F=9	G=16	H=3
I=13	J=2	K=7	L=12
M=11	N=8	O=1	P=14

Flowers for Algernon Word Search 1

```
N H L W P R O R S C H A C H C R S D R K
Y C C X K X D L X H C Z S Z R G T F E L
C T X L F V K K Z R T T L P G G R L P S
N K G G H R G I L D Z V C G D X A Y O P
F B P T E H Z T N S A K K Y V K U Y R B
W M D B P D B D Q N D L R X N B S O T Z
M A R T Z H B L O F I O I U F N S Z G D
H A R P T R W O C N T A R C C E K P U N
B N O R M A N V K A N D N S E E N Y A W
Y Z A O E O G E R A E E P V W P M R C
W M S G D N S O M T H Y R A B M K S I J
S S B R P S B L A D E Y R Y I E E I N D
T D O E Z A L R G K R G C G E W S Q O Z
E G W S L I O C N E E H B P E C F I Z
A Q L S L I N T K D B X A V R L A R T R
C W N G R N T A X I M P R M T B P A A C
H K X E E A B R W E E H L E S E E N R M
E B T D M A Q Q L D V Q I M R R M K E W
R E L Z M U L P V M O G E O F G J B P Q
D E K L H A R G N Z N V L R G Q Q F O N
S J G N Q X Z T E I X K S I Q C X M L D
X T B L V V N E C R N D Y E B V K V T R
T M P J T P Z N Y T N B W S P M M B V B
B D Q B W L A Q K P B O K S N J W N J X
J W P T N D C D W S G R N Y C D S W H X
```

Administered inkblot and other tests (6)
Algernon and Charlie competed at this (4)
Alice Kinnian's occupation (7)
Alice's last name (7)
An ordinary man trying to do a great man's work (5)
Author (5)
Charlie and Agernon did this in Chicago (6)
Charlie found them disturbing (6)
Charlie's condition at Mrs. Nemur's party (5)
Charlie's family name (6)
Charlie's father (4)
Charlie's feeling for Alice (4)
Charlie's increased (2)
Charlie's mother (4)
Charlie's pastime with Fay (7)
Charlie's sister (5)
College for Retarded Adults (7)
Date of last progress report; ___ 21st (8)
Dr. who treated Charlie like a human being (7)
Fay who was full of life and excitement (7)
Foundation that provided money for experiment (7)

He said he was as good as Charlie (5)
How Charlie's intelligence increased (9)
Inkblot test (9)
March 3 was the date of the first ___ report (8)
Mouse with increased intelligence (8)
Owner of bakery (6)
Psychiatrist and neurosurgeon (7)
Shop Matt wanted to own (6)
State Home and Training School (6)
Stole from Mr. Donner (5)
Teacher with whom Charlie fell in love (5)
They gradually returned to Charlie (8)
Vehicle for telling the story; progress ___ (6)
Wanted to be smart to have people like him (7)
What Charlie wanted to be (5)
What happened to Algernon (4)
What happened to artificially increased intelligence (12)
Where Charlie wanted flowers for Algernon (5)
Where Charlie worked (6)
Where experiments were done (10)

Flowers for Algernon Word Search 1 Answer Key

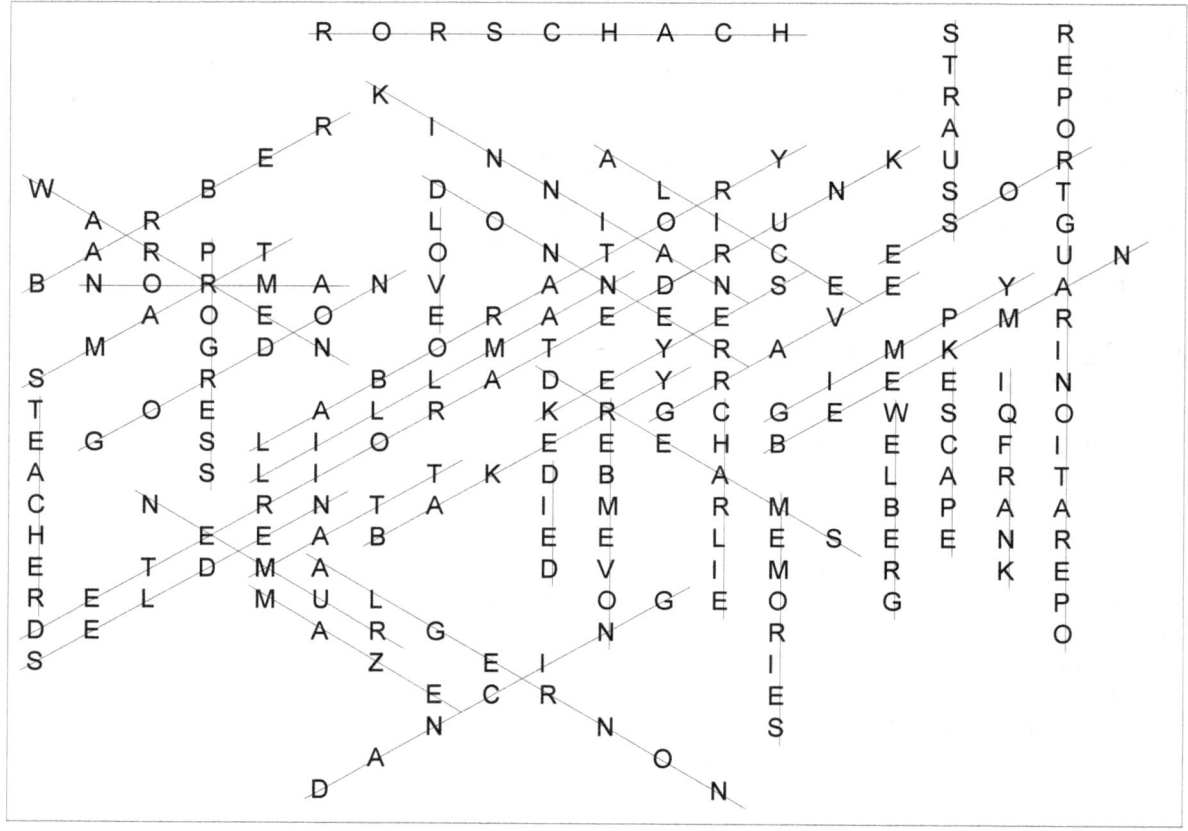

Administered inkblot and other tests (6)
Algernon and Charlie competed at this (4)
Alice Kinnian's occupation (7)
Alice's last name (7)
An ordinary man trying to do a great man's work (5)
Author (5)
Charlie and Agernon did this in Chicago (6)
Charlie found them disturbing (6)
Charlie's condition at Mrs. Nemur's party (5)
Charlie's family name (6)
Charlie's father (4)
Charlie's feeling for Alice (4)
Charlie's increased (2)
Charlie's mother (4)
Charlie's pastime with Fay (7)
Charlie's sister (5)
College for Retarded Adults (7)
Date of last progress report; ___ 21st (8)
Dr. who treated Charlie like a human being (7)
Fay who was full of life and excitement (7)
Foundation that provided money for experiment (7)
He said he was as good as Charlie (5)
How Charlie's intelligence increased (9)
Inkblot test (9)
March 3 was the date of the first ___ report (8)
Mouse with increased intelligence (8)
Owner of bakery (6)
Psychiatrist and neurosurgeon (7)
Shop Matt wanted to own (6)
State Home and Training School (6)
Stole from Mr. Donner (5)
Teacher with whom Charlie fell in love (5)
They gradually returned to Charlie (8)
Vehicle for telling the story; progress ___ (6)
Wanted to be smart to have people like him (7)
What Charlie wanted to be (5)
What happened to Algernon (4)
What happened to artificially increased intelligence (12)
Where Charlie wanted flowers for Algernon (5)
Where Charlie worked (6)
Where experiments were done (10)

Flowers for Algernon Word Search 2

```
S D E K C Y D V Q W S K P F V A Y W T B
M W V I V H V T Y D M N N V R M L Q Z R
C A O N I R A U G R A O P E R A T I O N
J R L N Q O C R E M R N V Q L Z N H C C
D R P I B S M H L M T A C G N E D K Y E
O E L A M E C L A I R D E I E S C A P E
N N T N Q A I P F G E R R B N B C Q B S
N W S E E L T P Q N N O R E J G N R S Q
E C E T R S D T N O P R D F A R U R S S
R B K L R I E I N P X S R N A M K E E B
K X E Y B A O L E B J C U T E C S I R V
N Z Y P Q E U R D D R H N N X G R X G V
Y R E K A B R S A E S A K Q R O I Y O T
Y D S B Q E E G S T N C P R M E R M R Z
B Q D Z B J B M X N E H S E K O P Z P G
N O D R O G M L Y B D D M B T M L O B Y
X R A C F B E V T H Y X H A V H N K R J
M B Z J C F V H R J R Y R P H N Y S Y T
B R W J J B O B T Q X O R K C M Z L R Q
G X G B B X N G B L B T V N W X X F P J
V D C F W W W Q L A V H B X K S S X T B
W P B C S N T R L V R M J R Y D F F W K
X K B Y F P Z G G K S Z S F G X T D D L
V Z C Q N F S T T N Z N Y D R L M X F Y
T B K C M T W F V S Z L N K M Q F Y H J
```

Administered inkblot and other tests (6)
Algernon and Charlie competed at this (4)
Alice Kinnian's occupation (7)
Alice's last name (7)
An ordinary man trying to do a great man's work (5)
Author (5)
Charlie and Agernon did this in Chicago (6)
Charlie found them disturbing (6)
Charlie's condition at Mrs. Nemur's party (5)
Charlie's family name (6)
Charlie's father (4)
Charlie's feeling for Alice (4)
Charlie's increased (2)
Charlie's mother (4)
Charlie's pastime with Fay (7)
Charlie's sister (5)
College for Retarded Adults (7)
Date of last progress report; ___ 21st (8)
Dr. who treated Charlie like a human being (7)
Fay who was full of life and excitement (7)
Foundation that provided money for experiment (7)

He said he was as good as Charlie (5)
How Charlie's intelligence increased (9)
Inkblot test (9)
March 3 was the date of the first ___ report (8)
Mouse with increased intelligence (8)
Owner of bakery (6)
Psychiatrist and neurosurgeon (7)
Shop Matt wanted to own (6)
State Home and Training School (6)
Stole from Mr. Donner (5)
Teacher with whom Charlie fell in love (5)
They gradually returned to Charlie (8)
Vehicle for telling the story; progress ___ (6)
Wanted to be smart to have people like him (7)
What Charlie wanted to be (5)
What happened to Algernon (4)
What happened to artificially increased intelligence (12)
Where Charlie wanted flowers for Algernon (5)
Where Charlie worked (6)
Where experiments were done (10)

Flowers for Algernon Word Search 2 Answer Key

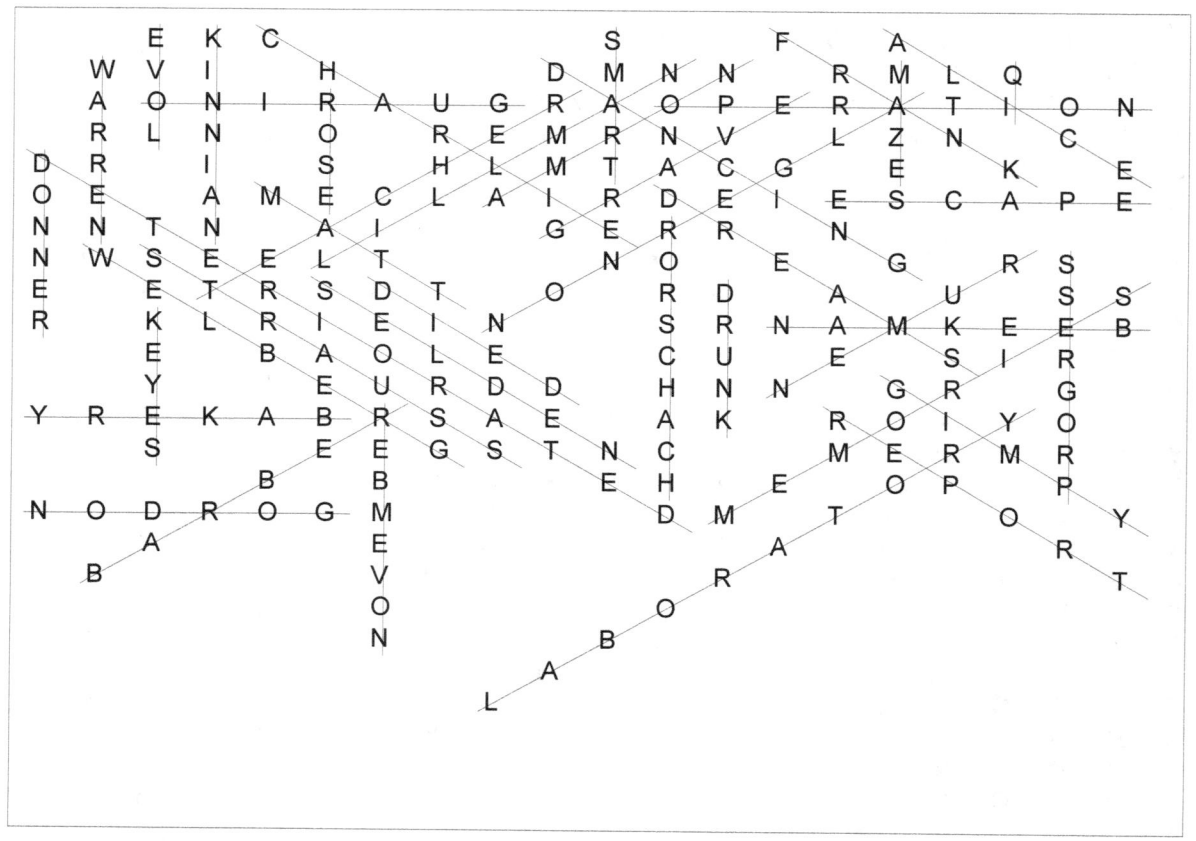

Administered inkblot and other tests (6)
Algernon and Charlie competed at this (4)
Alice Kinnian's occupation (7)
Alice's last name (7)
An ordinary man trying to do a great man's work (5)
Author (5)
Charlie and Agernon did this in Chicago (6)
Charlie found them disturbing (6)
Charlie's condition at Mrs. Nemur's party (5)
Charlie's family name (6)
Charlie's father (4)
Charlie's feeling for Alice (4)
Charlie's increased (2)
Charlie's mother (4)
Charlie's pastime with Fay (7)
Charlie's sister (5)
College for Retarded Adults (7)
Date of last progress report; ___ 21st (8)
Dr. who treated Charlie like a human being (7)
Fay who was full of life and excitement (7)
Foundation that provided money for experiment (7)
He said he was as good as Charlie (5)
How Charlie's intelligence increased (9)
Inkblot test (9)
March 3 was the date of the first ___ report (8)
Mouse with increased intelligence (8)
Owner of bakery (6)
Psychiatrist and neurosurgeon (7)
Shop Matt wanted to own (6)
State Home and Training School (6)
Stole from Mr. Donner (5)
Teacher with whom Charlie fell in love (5)
They gradually returned to Charlie (8)
Vehicle for telling the story; progress ___ (6)
Wanted to be smart to have people like him (7)
What Charlie wanted to be (5)
What happened to Algernon (4)
What happened to artificially increased intelligence (12)
Where Charlie wanted flowers for Algernon (5)
Where Charlie worked (6)
Where experiments were done (10)

Flowers for Algernon Word Search 3

```
D E T E R I O R A T E D M Z S X P Q X C
B G K L K Q K T L A B O R A T O R Y F Q
V W L F W K V L H B N M R L C H B G C T
Q G Y M N B P T N K Q H E T W W Z R W R
B Q M C D D C F O S N G B J D T B M P M
R R K Q W O X E I J A O M E L B Y E L F
T G Y H M N B P T V M R E M E N Q I W M
V F P L L N N A A K L D V X G K T L K N
D J M W F E F C R L L O O B R T M R P C
A D I E D R O S E K I N N I A N M A Z E
N X G L A R E E P Q L C V M V R L H N V
C T E N T I U S O X L D E V E G B C Q A
I S K W R X K N L R J N L G E Y T E M X
N Y S O B R E S K L O V E R T Q D R R D
G E M L R R Y M D N R R N N E K O E S F
D E M C Q R E A I M W O S N A N Y P X W
M H Q U H F S R P R N F D C C V B O H F
B A K E R Y A T Y R S P T L H W K R J F
R W C M F U W S R M O C F G E A X T S H
L W X W G H P E A A S G S P R P C W S J
D Z V F Z S W E L V U B R R S K S H F M
W Z P W B Z R N R B T S N E R R A W R N
F H V K Z D Q B F L E F S S S Z M J L G
H H Q W D V S T Z M W R K K S S L Y R G
D C L F H H Y K R F X G G J Q K R L C M
```

ALGERNON	DRUNK	LILLMAN	RORSCHACH
ALICE	ESCAPE	LOVE	ROSE
BAKERY	FRANK	MATT	SELDEN
BARBER	GIMPY	MAZE	SMART
BEEKMAN	GORDON	MEMORIES	STRAUSS
CHARLIE	GRAVE	NEMUR	TEACHER
DANCING	GUARINO	NORMA	WARREN
DETERIORATED	IQ	NOVEMBER	WELBERG
DIED	KEYES	OPERATION	
DONNER	KINNIAN	PROGRESS	
DREAMS	LABORATORY	REPORT	

Flowers for Algernon Word Search 3 Answer Key

```
D E T E R I O R A T E D
            L A B O R A T O R Y
                            R
              N       N  G  E
          D   O       A  O  B          E
          O   I   E   M  R  M      E   I
      Y   N   T   P   L  D  E      K T M   L
  D   P   N   A   A   L  O  V   B  R N M   R
D A I E D R O S E K I N N I A N M   Z E
A N G L R E E Q L C   M V E G B   C N
N C K   R I K P   R   E E T E   O A
C I S   O K E N   O   R T A M R
N N E   M Y M I   N   S C H E
G E M   U S A P   S     H R
M B A K E R Y A T R     E A
            U W R M O   R C
          G   E A U G   H
              E L S N E R R A W
          D   R   B S   S
                  E     S
                  R
                  G
```

ALGERNON DRUNK LILLMAN RORSCHACH

ALICE ESCAPE LOVE ROSE

BAKERY FRANK MATT SELDEN

BARBER GIMPY MAZE SMART

BEEKMAN GORDON MEMORIES STRAUSS

CHARLIE GRAVE NEMUR TEACHER

DANCING GUARINO NORMA WARREN

DETERIORATED IQ NOVEMBER WELBERG

DIED KEYES OPERATION

DONNER KINNIAN PROGRESS

DREAMS LABORATORY REPORT

Flowers for Algernon Word Search 4

```
M D C Q V B M N D W Q H N J M C Q D D C
E V I W Y Y Z C E B O K D H M A Y G T E X
M A K E Y E S K I N N I A N Z Y T D T J
O L Y C D C E L S Q A N C O E A R R E Q
R I N W A N L A Y S T R E N M L A E R Y
I C T P E O D B W T F C B R Y O M A I Y
E E E V N R E O G R E B L E W V S M O Q
S L A Q E M N R I A O W M G X E W S R X
P R Y B M A X A M U B S Z L J J S G A K
G R R G U G B T P S S A E A D C Q N T M
J A O O R B O O Y S W I K L P R N I E J
B Y N G N F R Q R L A I E E F U C D X
N G I D R S O Y D R Y L R P R F Z N P S
Y S R Z Y E C V A O L G O R Q Y J A K M
Y D A Z G T S H E M N R D B E Y X D M H
X S U Z V E C S A M T L F Y E N R S J J
K N G N R A N N L C B Y X Q F E X L M H
Z G T N D C M O Z V H E V G Z R K F T J
X C X M J H M I M Y L P R M W F G M J T
Y R V M C E D T W S X L H B B R W D A W
Z Q Y Z S R N A L J T M X P L S K X F N
Y R J R N G K R V S Q J X B D P K C N V
C V Z K V Y P E L P C J V N N W R Z X K
V R M X P H D P R B K T B V X T P F F H
Z F W Z Z L M O C S D Z D S K W Y T W G
```

ALGERNON	DRUNK	LILLMAN	RORSCHACH
ALICE	ESCAPE	LOVE	ROSE
BAKERY	FRANK	MATT	SELDEN
BARBER	GIMPY	MAZE	SMART
BEEKMAN	GORDON	MEMORIES	STRAUSS
CHARLIE	GRAVE	NEMUR	TEACHER
DANCING	GUARINO	NORMA	WARREN
DETERIORATED	IQ	NOVEMBER	WELBERG
DIED	KEYES	OPERATION	
DONNER	KINNIAN	PROGRESS	
DREAMS	LABORATORY	REPORT	

Flowers for Algernon Word Search 4 Answer Key

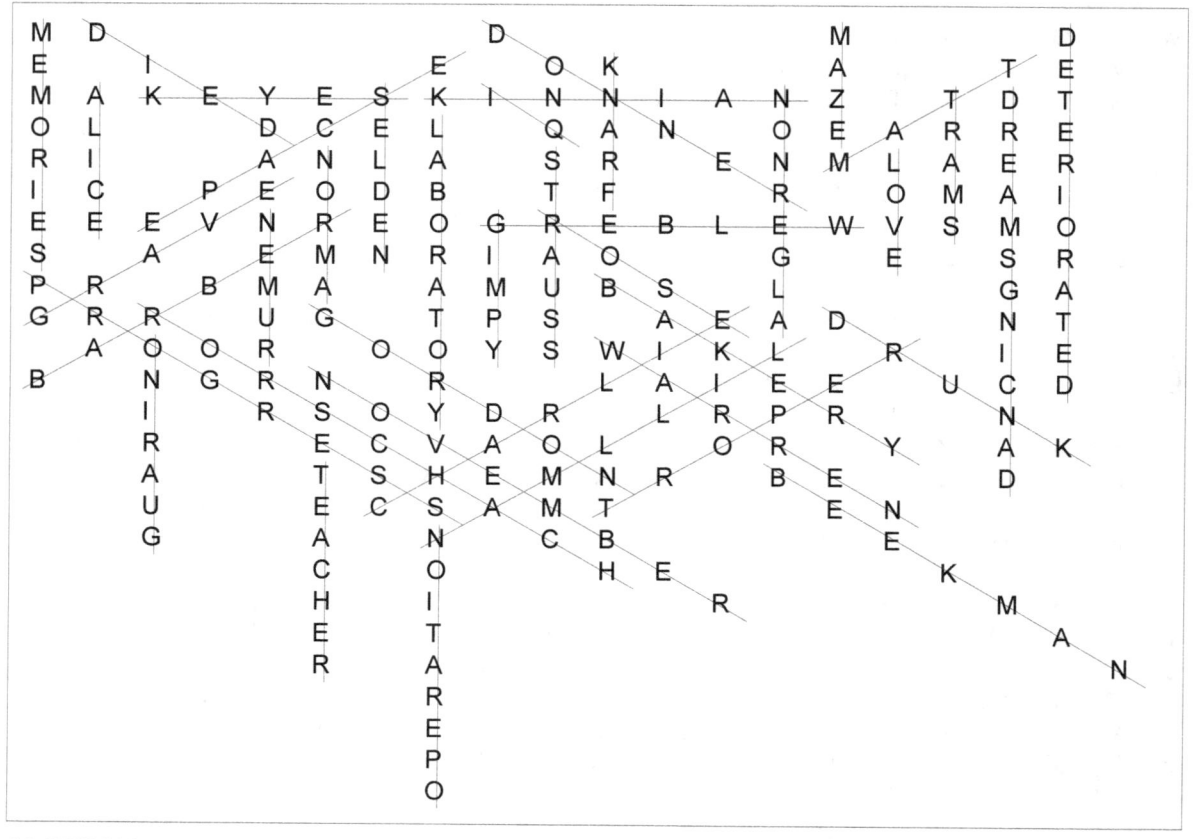

ALGERNON	DRUNK	LILLMAN	RORSCHACH
ALICE	ESCAPE	LOVE	ROSE
BAKERY	FRANK	MATT	SELDEN
BARBER	GIMPY	MAZE	SMART
BEEKMAN	GORDON	MEMORIES	STRAUSS
CHARLIE	GRAVE	NEMUR	TEACHER
DANCING	GUARINO	NORMA	WARREN
DETERIORATED	IQ	NOVEMBER	WELBERG
DIED	KEYES	OPERATION	
DONNER	KINNIAN	PROGRESS	
DREAMS	LABORATORY	REPORT	

Flowers for Algernon Crossword 1

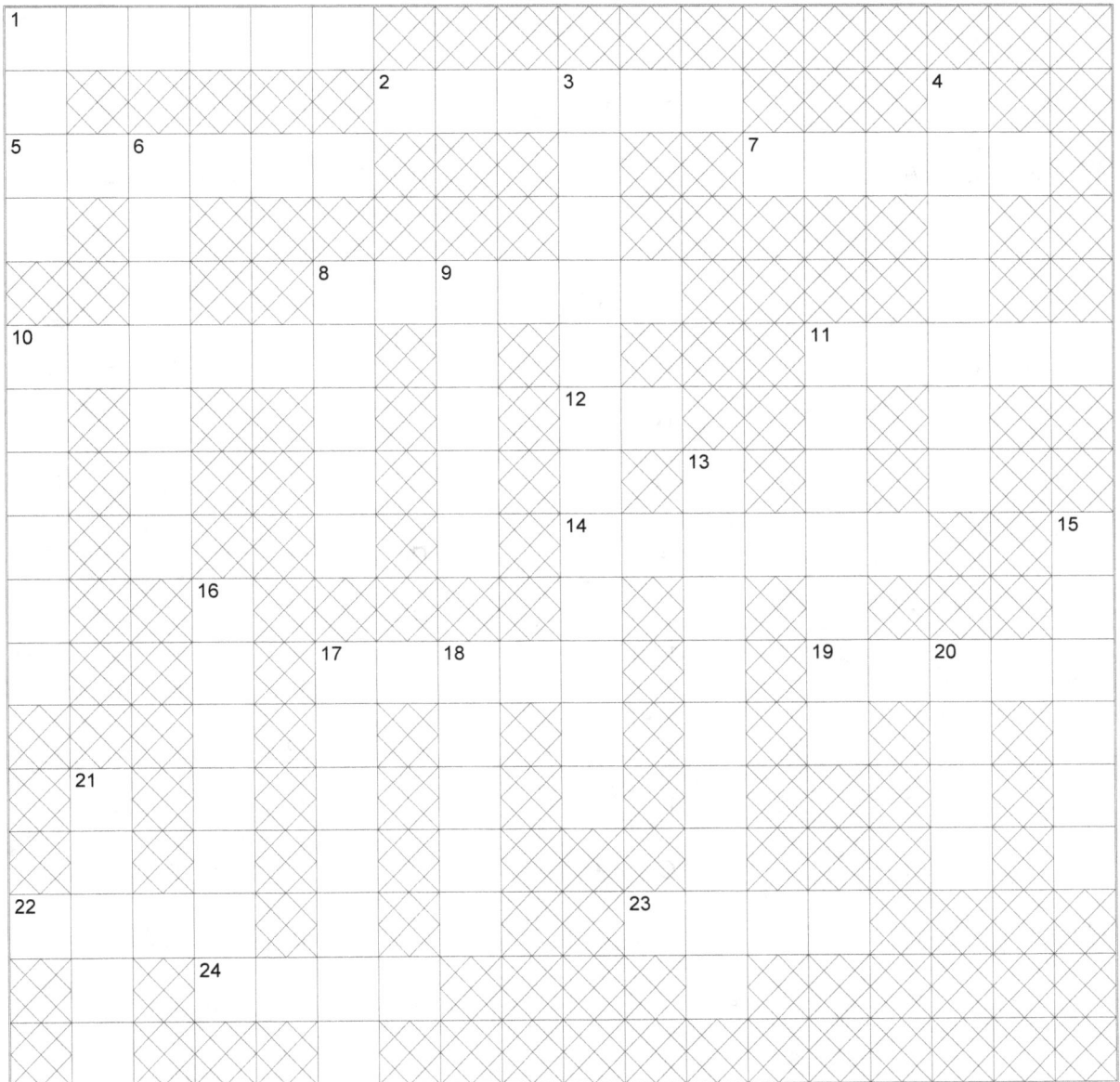

Across
1. Charlie found them disturbing
2. Administered inkblot and other tests
5. Charlie and Agernon did this in Chicago
7. Author
8. Owner of bakery
10. Shop Matt wanted to own
11. Stole from Mr. Donner
12. Charlie's increased
14. Vehicle for telling the story; progress ___
17. What Charlie wanted to be
19. An ordinary man trying to do a great man's work
22. Algernon and Charlie competed at this
23. Charlie's feeling for Alice
24. Charlie's mother

Down
1. What happened to Algernon
3. What happened to artificially increased intelligence
4. College for Retarded Adults
6. Wanted to be smart to have people like him
8. Charlie's condition at Mrs. Nemur's party
9. Charlie's sister
10. Where Charlie worked
11. Dr. who treated Charlie like a human being
13. How Charlie's intelligence increased
15. Charlie's family name
16. Alice Kinnian's occupation
17. Psychiatrist and neurosurgeon
18. Teacher with whom Charlie fell in love
20. Charlie's father
21. He said he was as good as Charlie

Flowers for Algernon Crossword 1 Answer Key

	1 D	R	E	A	M	S								
	I				2 S	E	L	3 D	E	N		4 B		
5 E	S	6 C	A	P	E			E		7 K	E	Y	E	S
	D		H					T				E		
			A		8 D	9 O	N	N	E	R		K		
10 B	A	R	B	E	R		O			R		11 G	I	M	P	Y
A		L			U		R		12 I	Q		U		A
K		I			N		M		O		13 O		A		N
E		E			K		A		14 R	E	P	O	R	T		15 G
R				16 T					A		E		I		O
Y				E		17 S	M	18 A	R	T		R		19 N	E	20 M	U	R
				A		T		L		E		A		O		A		D
		21 F		C		R		I		D		T				T		O
		R		H		A		C		I						T		N
22 M	A	Z	E			U		E		23 L	O	V	E		
		N		24 R	O	S	E			N					
		K				S									

Across
1. Charlie found them disturbing
2. Administered inkblot and other tests
5. Charlie and Agernon did this in Chicago
7. Author
8. Owner of bakery
10. Shop Matt wanted to own
11. Stole from Mr. Donner
12. Charlie's increased
14. Vehicle for telling the story; progress ___
17. What Charlie wanted to be
19. An ordinary man trying to do a great man's work
22. Algernon and Charlie competed at this
23. Charlie's feeling for Alice
24. Charlie's mother

Down
1. What happened to Algernon
3. What happened to artificially increased intelligence
4. College for Retarded Adults
6. Wanted to be smart to have people like him
8. Charlie's condition at Mrs. Nemur's party
9. Charlie's sister
10. Where Charlie worked
11. Dr. who treated Charlie like a human being
13. How Charlie's intelligence increased
15. Charlie's family name
16. Alice Kinnian's occupation
17. Psychiatrist and neurosurgeon
18. Teacher with whom Charlie fell in love
20. Charlie's father
21. He said he was as good as Charlie

Flowers for Algernon Crossword 2

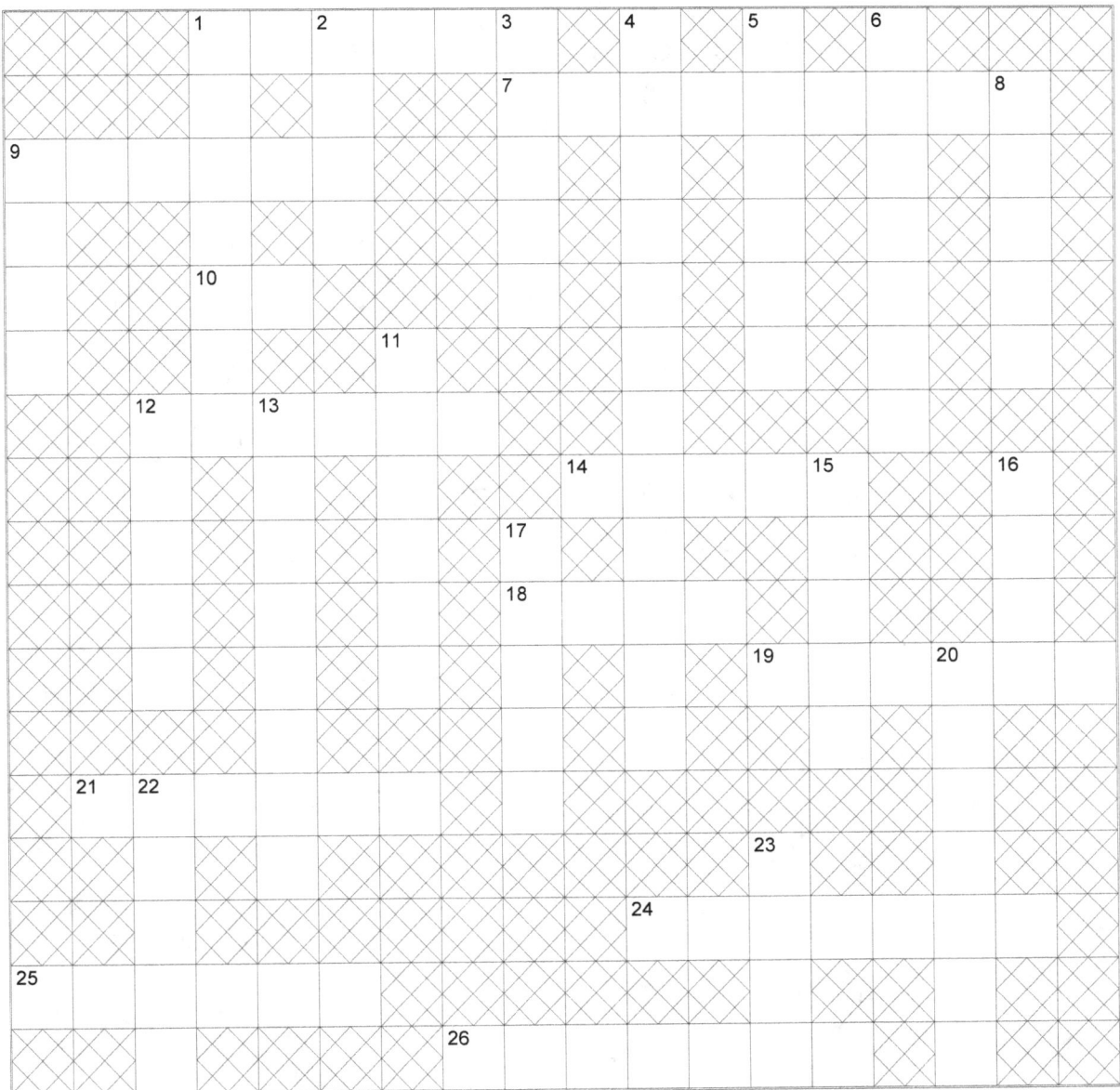

Across
1. Charlie's family name
7. How Charlie's intelligence increased
9. Charlie found them disturbing
10. Charlie's increased
12. Owner of bakery
14. He said he was as good as Charlie
18. Charlie's father
19. Administered inkblot and other tests
21. Where Charlie worked
24. Wanted to be smart to have people like him
25. Charlie and Agernon did this in Chicago
26. Alice Kinnian's occupation

Down
1. Dr. who treated Charlie like a human being
2. Charlie's mother
3. Charlie's sister
4. What happened to artificially increased intelligence
5. Shop Matt wanted to own
6. Alice's last name
8. An ordinary man trying to do a great man's work
9. What happened to Algernon
11. Vehicle for telling the story; progress ___
12. Charlie's condition at Mrs. Nemur's party
13. Date of last progress report; ___ 21st
15. Author
16. Charlie's feeling for Alice
17. What Charlie wanted to be
20. Charlie's pastime with Fay
22. Teacher with whom Charlie fell in love
23. Algernon and Charlie competed at this

Flowers for Algernon Crossword 2 Answer Key

			1 G	2 O	3 R	D	O	4 N		5 D		6 B		K	
			U		O			7 O	P	E	R	A	T	I	8 N
9 D	R	E	A	M	S			R		T		R		N	E
I			R	E				M		E		B		N	M
E			10 I	Q				A		R		E		I	U
D			N			11 R		I		R		A			R
		12 D	13 N	N	E	R			O			N		
			R	O		P			14 F	R	A	15 K		16 L	
			U				17 S	A			E		O	
			N	E		R		18 M	A	T	T		Y		V
			K	M				A		E		19 S	E	20 L	D	E	N
				B				R		D		S		A	
	21 B	22 A	K	E	R	Y			T					N	
		L		R							23 M		C	
		I						24 C	H	A	R	L	I	E
25 E	S	C	A	P	E						Z		N	
		E			26 T	E	A	C	H	E	R		G	

Across
1. Charlie's family name
7. How Charlie's intelligence increased
9. Charlie found them disturbing
10. Charlie's increased
12. Owner of bakery
14. He said he was as good as Charlie
18. Charlie's father
19. Administered inkblot and other tests
21. Where Charlie worked
24. Wanted to be smart to have people like him
25. Charlie and Agernon did this in Chicago
26. Alice Kinnian's occupation

Down
1. Dr. who treated Charlie like a human being
2. Charlie's mother
3. Charlie's sister
4. What happened to artificially increased intelligence
5. Shop Matt wanted to own
6. Alice's last name
8. An ordinary man trying to do a great man's work
9. What happened to Algernon
11. Vehicle for telling the story; progress ___
12. Charlie's condition at Mrs. Nemur's party
13. Date of last progress report; ___ 21st
15. Author
16. Charlie's feeling for Alice
17. What Charlie wanted to be
20. Charlie's pastime with Fay
22. Teacher with whom Charlie fell in love
23. Algernon and Charlie competed at this

Flowers for Algernon Crossword 3

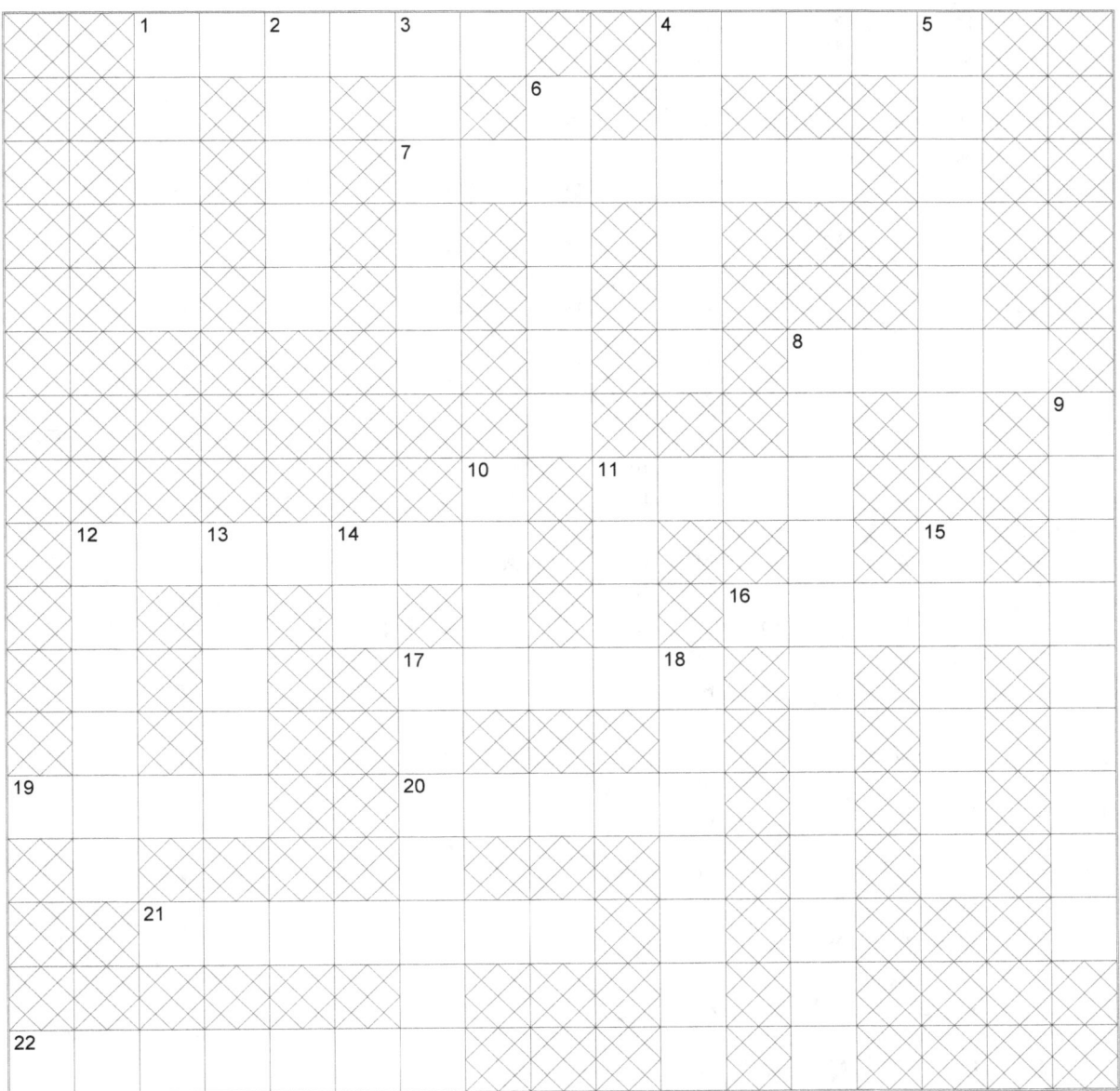

Across
1. Owner of bakery
4. What Charlie wanted to be
7. Wanted to be smart to have people like him
8. What happened to Algernon
11. Charlie's father
12. Dr. who treated Charlie like a human being
16. Charlie found them disturbing
17. Author
19. Charlie's mother
20. An ordinary man trying to do a great man's work
21. Charlie's pastime with Fay
22. College for Retarded Adults

Down
1. Charlie's condition at Mrs. Nemur's party
2. Charlie's sister
3. Charlie and Agernon did this in Chicago
4. Administered inkblot and other tests
5. Alice Kinnian's occupation
6. Shop Matt wanted to own
8. What happened to artificially increased intelligence
9. Inkblot test
10. Charlie's feeling for Alice
11. Algernon and Charlie competed at this
12. Charlie's family name
13. Teacher with whom Charlie fell in love
14. Charlie's increased
15. Where Charlie worked
17. Alice's last name
18. Psychiatrist and neurosurgeon

Flowers for Algernon Crossword 3 Answer Key

Across
1. Owner of bakery
4. What Charlie wanted to be
7. Wanted to be smart to have people like him
8. What happened to Algernon
11. Charlie's father
12. Dr. who treated Charlie like a human being
16. Charlie found them disturbing
17. Author
19. Charlie's mother
20. An ordinary man trying to do a great man's work
21. Charlie's pastime with Fay
22. College for Retarded Adults

Down
1. Charlie's condition at Mrs. Nemur's party
2. Charlie's sister
3. Charlie and Agernon did this in Chicago
4. Administered inkblot and other tests
5. Alice Kinnian's occupation
6. Shop Matt wanted to own
8. What happened to artificially increased intelligence
9. Inkblot test
10. Charlie's feeling for Alice
11. Algernon and Charlie competed at this
12. Charlie's family name
13. Teacher with whom Charlie fell in love
14. Charlie's increased
15. Where Charlie worked
17. Alice's last name
18. Psychiatrist and neurosurgeon

Flowers for Algernon Crossword 4

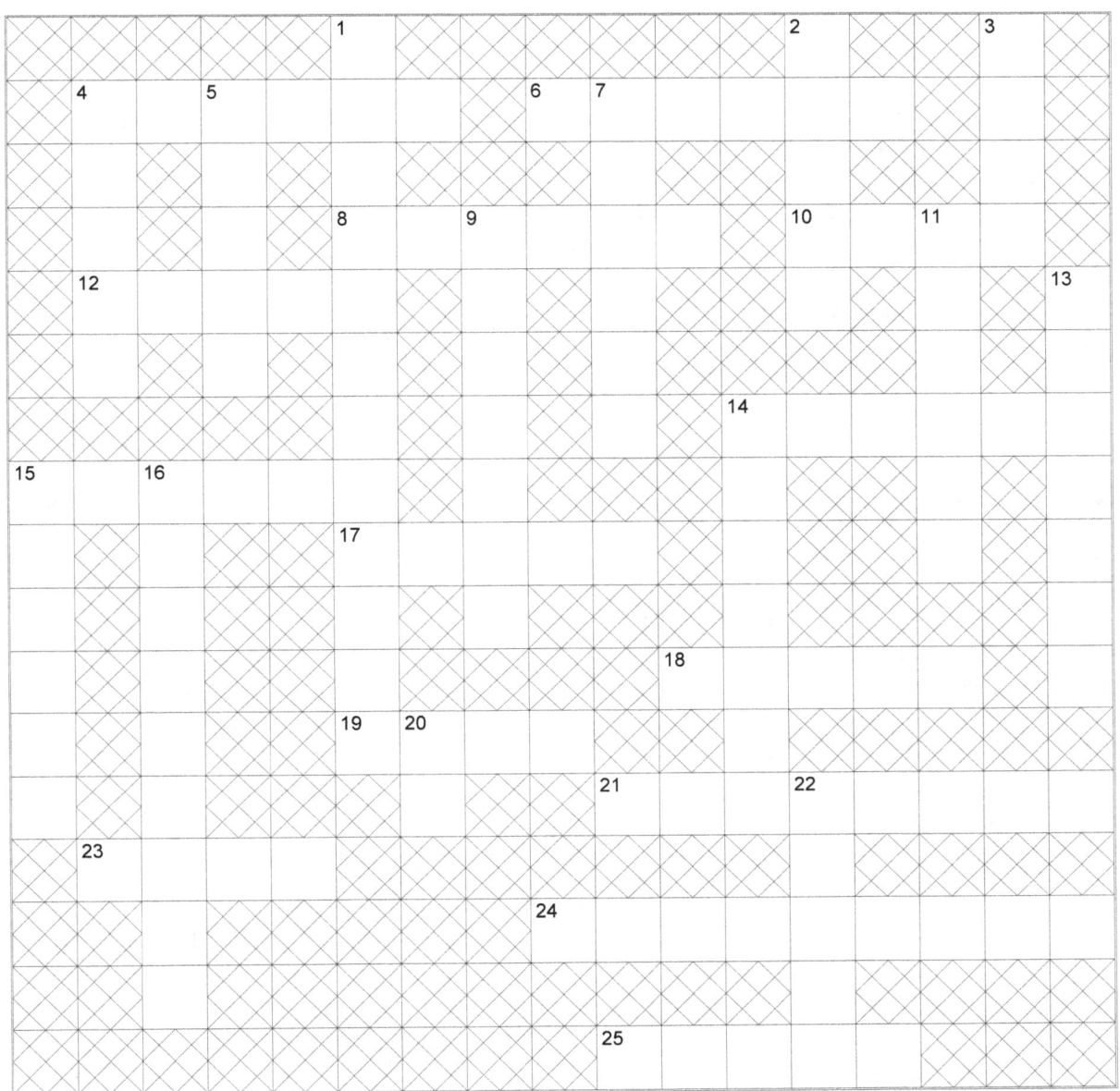

Across
- 4. Owner of bakery
- 6. Charlie found them disturbing
- 8. Charlie and Agernon did this in Chicago
- 10. Charlie's mother
- 12. An ordinary man trying to do a great man's work
- 14. Charlie's family name
- 15. Shop Matt wanted to own
- 17. Teacher with whom Charlie fell in love
- 18. Stole from Mr. Donner
- 19. What happened to Algernon
- 21. March 3 was the date of the first ___ report
- 23. Charlie's father
- 24. How Charlie's intelligence increased
- 25. Author

Down
- 1. What happened to artificially increased intelligence
- 2. What Charlie wanted to be
- 3. Charlie's feeling for Alice
- 4. Charlie's condition at Mrs. Nemur's party
- 5. Charlie's sister
- 7. Vehicle for telling the story; progress ___
- 9. Wanted to be smart to have people like him
- 11. Administered inkblot and other tests
- 13. Alice's last name
- 14. Dr. who treated Charlie like a human being
- 15. Where Charlie worked
- 16. Inkblot test
- 20. Charlie's increased
- 22. Where Charlie wanted flowers for Algernon

Flowers for Algernon Crossword 4 Answer Key

Across
4. Owner of bakery
6. Charlie found them disturbing
8. Charlie and Agernon did this in Chicago
10. Charlie's mother
12. An ordinary man trying to do a great man's work
14. Charlie's family name
15. Shop Matt wanted to own
17. Teacher with whom Charlie fell in love
18. Stole from Mr. Donner
19. What happened to Algernon
21. March 3 was the date of the first ___ report
23. Charlie's father
24. How Charlie's intelligence increased
25. Author

Down
1. What happened to artificially increased intelligence
2. What Charlie wanted to be
3. Charlie's feeling for Alice
4. Charlie's condition at Mrs. Nemur's party
5. Charlie's sister
7. Vehicle for telling the story; progress ___
9. Wanted to be smart to have people like him
11. Administered inkblot and other tests
13. Alice's last name
14. Dr. who treated Charlie like a human being
15. Where Charlie worked
16. Inkblot test
20. Charlie's increased
22. Where Charlie wanted flowers for Algernon

Flowers for Algernon

LABORATORY	GIMPY	DRUNK	TEACHER	ALICE
NOVEMBER	DETERIORATED	LOVE	LILLMAN	BARBER
RORSCHACH	NEMUR	FREE SPACE	SMART	ALGERNON
ROSE	KEYES	GORDON	DANCING	OPERATION
MAZE	SELDEN	MEMORIES	WELBERG	ESCAPE

Flowers for Algernon

KINNIAN	BAKERY	IQ	FRANK	WARREN
GUARINO	STRAUSS	CHARLIE	DREAMS	REPORT
MATT	NORMA	FREE SPACE	GRAVE	BEEKMAN
DIED	ESCAPE	WELBERG	MEMORIES	SELDEN
MAZE	OPERATION	DANCING	GORDON	KEYES

Flowers for Algernon

MATT	DIED	ALGERNON	DREAMS	ALICE
OPERATION	GUARINO	LABORATORY	BEEKMAN	STRAUSS
GIMPY	LOVE	FREE SPACE	ESCAPE	DRUNK
REPORT	GRAVE	CHARLIE	TEACHER	BAKERY
BARBER	MEMORIES	NEMUR	LILLMAN	IQ

Flowers for Algernon

ROSE	DANCING	SELDEN	KINNIAN	WELBERG
NOVEMBER	GORDON	PROGRESS	KEYES	DONNER
DETERIORATED	MAZE	FREE SPACE	FRANK	WARREN
SMART	IQ	LILLMAN	NEMUR	MEMORIES
BARBER	BAKERY	TEACHER	CHARLIE	GRAVE

Flowers for Algernon

WARREN	TEACHER	NEMUR	DONNER	ESCAPE
NORMA	RORSCHACH	PROGRESS	LOVE	DREAMS
GORDON	KEYES	FREE SPACE	REPORT	LABORATORY
WELBERG	OPERATION	IQ	CHARLIE	DIED
ALICE	BEEKMAN	GUARINO	ROSE	KINNIAN

Flowers for Algernon

GIMPY	FRANK	SMART	DETERIORATED	BARBER
BAKERY	NOVEMBER	MAZE	MATT	LILLMAN
SELDEN	ALGERNON	FREE SPACE	STRAUSS	MEMORIES
DRUNK	KINNIAN	ROSE	GUARINO	BEEKMAN
ALICE	DIED	CHARLIE	IQ	OPERATION

Flowers for Algernon

ROSE	LILLMAN	WELBERG	DREAMS	MAZE
DONNER	FRANK	NORMA	LABORATORY	BEEKMAN
ALICE	KEYES	FREE SPACE	STRAUSS	NOVEMBER
SELDEN	RORSCHACH	MATT	GORDON	DIED
ALGERNON	CHARLIE	REPORT	GUARINO	GIMPY

Flowers for Algernon

KINNIAN	BARBER	BAKERY	DETERIORATED	WARREN
LOVE	DRUNK	PROGRESS	OPERATION	SMART
TEACHER	DANCING	FREE SPACE	IQ	NEMUR
GRAVE	GIMPY	GUARINO	REPORT	CHARLIE
ALGERNON	DIED	GORDON	MATT	RORSCHACH

Flowers for Algernon

DANCING	DONNER	ROSE	NOVEMBER	RORSCHACH
DRUNK	MAZE	BEEKMAN	KINNIAN	BARBER
MATT	ALICE	FREE SPACE	DREAMS	ESCAPE
BAKERY	LILLMAN	DIED	DETERIORATED	LABORATORY
STRAUSS	LOVE	SMART	GRAVE	CHARLIE

Flowers for Algernon

KEYES	WARREN	ALGERNON	SELDEN	TEACHER
MEMORIES	NEMUR	FRANK	IQ	WELBERG
OPERATION	PROGRESS	FREE SPACE	GORDON	REPORT
GUARINO	CHARLIE	GRAVE	SMART	LOVE
STRAUSS	LABORATORY	DETERIORATED	DIED	LILLMAN

Flowers for Algernon

DONNER	LABORATORY	ROSE	FRANK	SMART
NEMUR	PROGRESS	NORMA	WARREN	CHARLIE
ESCAPE	TEACHER	FREE SPACE	BEEKMAN	DANCING
DRUNK	LOVE	OPERATION	GUARINO	ALGERNON
GIMPY	WELBERG	REPORT	BAKERY	RORSCHACH

Flowers for Algernon

MAZE	IQ	DETERIORATED	STRAUSS	DIED
KEYES	GRAVE	LILLMAN	MATT	GORDON
DREAMS	NOVEMBER	FREE SPACE	ALICE	MEMORIES
BARBER	RORSCHACH	BAKERY	REPORT	WELBERG
GIMPY	ALGERNON	GUARINO	OPERATION	LOVE

Flowers for Algernon

NORMA	STRAUSS	PROGRESS	LOVE	GUARINO
ALGERNON	ESCAPE	CHARLIE	OPERATION	GIMPY
GORDON	NOVEMBER	FREE SPACE	SELDEN	DONNER
LABORATORY	MEMORIES	NEMUR	ALICE	MAZE
DETERIORATED	FRANK	RORSCHACH	DREAMS	GRAVE

Flowers for Algernon

ROSE	WARREN	REPORT	DRUNK	DANCING
KEYES	BARBER	SMART	KINNIAN	LILLMAN
BAKERY	BEEKMAN	FREE SPACE	IQ	TEACHER
WELBERG	GRAVE	DREAMS	RORSCHACH	FRANK
DETERIORATED	MAZE	ALICE	NEMUR	MEMORIES

Flowers for Algernon

ESCAPE	BEEKMAN	SELDEN	KINNIAN	OPERATION
LILLMAN	DRUNK	DANCING	GUARINO	PROGRESS
LOVE	NORMA	FREE SPACE	DONNER	DREAMS
WARREN	MEMORIES	DETERIORATED	BARBER	LABORATORY
SMART	WELBERG	TEACHER	NEMUR	ROSE

Flowers for Algernon

FRANK	STRAUSS	BAKERY	ALICE	GIMPY
KEYES	GORDON	ALGERNON	DIED	IQ
RORSCHACH	CHARLIE	FREE SPACE	MATT	GRAVE
NOVEMBER	ROSE	NEMUR	TEACHER	WELBERG
SMART	LABORATORY	BARBER	DETERIORATED	MEMORIES

Flowers for Algernon

KEYES	LABORATORY	ROSE	RORSCHACH	SELDEN
DANCING	NOVEMBER	MATT	TEACHER	SMART
IQ	GRAVE	FREE SPACE	CHARLIE	WARREN
ALGERNON	GIMPY	NORMA	NEMUR	STRAUSS
LOVE	OPERATION	BEEKMAN	WELBERG	BAKERY

Flowers for Algernon

GUARINO	ALICE	REPORT	BARBER	DIED
DRUNK	MAZE	DREAMS	DETERIORATED	GORDON
MEMORIES	KINNIAN	FREE SPACE	ESCAPE	PROGRESS
DONNER	BAKERY	WELBERG	BEEKMAN	OPERATION
LOVE	STRAUSS	NEMUR	NORMA	GIMPY

Flowers for Algernon

TEACHER	DRUNK	DANCING	NOVEMBER	LOVE
REPORT	MEMORIES	GRAVE	IQ	ROSE
MAZE	STRAUSS	FREE SPACE	KEYES	PROGRESS
DONNER	GORDON	DREAMS	DETERIORATED	WARREN
KINNIAN	OPERATION	NORMA	NEMUR	RORSCHACH

Flowers for Algernon

DIED	LABORATORY	GUARINO	SELDEN	WELBERG
ALICE	ALGERNON	LILLMAN	ESCAPE	BAKERY
FRANK	SMART	FREE SPACE	CHARLIE	BARBER
BEEKMAN	RORSCHACH	NEMUR	NORMA	OPERATION
KINNIAN	WARREN	DETERIORATED	DREAMS	GORDON

Flowers for Algernon

NEMUR	DIED	STRAUSS	BEEKMAN	CHARLIE
KEYES	GORDON	DREAMS	IQ	WELBERG
ALGERNON	ESCAPE	FREE SPACE	OPERATION	TEACHER
WARREN	PROGRESS	MAZE	LABORATORY	REPORT
GIMPY	NOVEMBER	MEMORIES	NORMA	LILLMAN

Flowers for Algernon

ROSE	DETERIORATED	FRANK	LOVE	ALICE
BAKERY	SELDEN	KINNIAN	BARBER	DANCING
SMART	GUARINO	FREE SPACE	DONNER	RORSCHACH
MATT	LILLMAN	NORMA	MEMORIES	NOVEMBER
GIMPY	REPORT	LABORATORY	MAZE	PROGRESS

Flowers for Algernon

WELBERG	ALGERNON	PROGRESS	IQ	NORMA
MAZE	ROSE	BEEKMAN	DREAMS	DRUNK
TEACHER	STRAUSS	FREE SPACE	LILLMAN	ESCAPE
OPERATION	KEYES	WARREN	DETERIORATED	GRAVE
BAKERY	DANCING	CHARLIE	LOVE	SMART

Flowers for Algernon

BARBER	DIED	LABORATORY	DONNER	ALICE
NEMUR	KINNIAN	RORSCHACH	MEMORIES	MATT
GORDON	GUARINO	FREE SPACE	REPORT	NOVEMBER
SELDEN	SMART	LOVE	CHARLIE	DANCING
BAKERY	GRAVE	DETERIORATED	WARREN	KEYES

Flowers for Algernon

ALICE	MEMORIES	STRAUSS	NORMA	BEEKMAN
BARBER	GORDON	BAKERY	SMART	GIMPY
DANCING	DONNER	FREE SPACE	CHARLIE	NEMUR
ALGERNON	WELBERG	OPERATION	PROGRESS	ROSE
DREAMS	KEYES	MATT	SELDEN	IQ

Flowers for Algernon

NOVEMBER	WARREN	ESCAPE	KINNIAN	DETERIORATED
RORSCHACH	REPORT	LOVE	DIED	MAZE
GUARINO	LILLMAN	FREE SPACE	LABORATORY	FRANK
DRUNK	IQ	SELDEN	MATT	KEYES
DREAMS	ROSE	PROGRESS	OPERATION	WELBERG

Flowers for Algernon

DRUNK	RORSCHACH	BARBER	ALGERNON	DONNER
TEACHER	KEYES	SELDEN	KINNIAN	LOVE
ESCAPE	DIED	FREE SPACE	GRAVE	DREAMS
NEMUR	ALICE	DETERIORATED	DANCING	LABORATORY
MATT	MAZE	OPERATION	GORDON	SMART

Flowers for Algernon

BAKERY	BEEKMAN	PROGRESS	IQ	ROSE
GUARINO	GIMPY	MEMORIES	FRANK	CHARLIE
NORMA	LILLMAN	FREE SPACE	REPORT	WELBERG
STRAUSS	SMART	GORDON	OPERATION	MAZE
MATT	LABORATORY	DANCING	DETERIORATED	ALICE

Flowers for Algernon

DIED	MATT	ALICE	TEACHER	DANCING
OPERATION	KINNIAN	NORMA	CHARLIE	ROSE
SMART	ALGERNON	FREE SPACE	DONNER	GUARINO
MEMORIES	LOVE	GRAVE	MAZE	SELDEN
NEMUR	LILLMAN	RORSCHACH	DRUNK	DETERIORATED

Flowers for Algernon

KEYES	BAKERY	BEEKMAN	REPORT	GORDON
BARBER	FRANK	WARREN	ESCAPE	WELBERG
IQ	GIMPY	FREE SPACE	NOVEMBER	PROGRESS
DREAMS	DETERIORATED	DRUNK	RORSCHACH	LILLMAN
NEMUR	SELDEN	MAZE	GRAVE	LOVE

Flowers for Algernon

KEYES	RORSCHACH	BARBER	DIED	ALICE
DRUNK	BAKERY	GORDON	GUARINO	NOVEMBER
GRAVE	OPERATION	FREE SPACE	DREAMS	IQ
TEACHER	NORMA	PROGRESS	ESCAPE	DONNER
REPORT	KINNIAN	WARREN	SELDEN	MATT

Flowers for Algernon

ROSE	DETERIORATED	NEMUR	SMART	FRANK
STRAUSS	CHARLIE	LILLMAN	LABORATORY	WELBERG
BEEKMAN	GIMPY	FREE SPACE	DANCING	ALGERNON
MAZE	MATT	SELDEN	WARREN	KINNIAN
REPORT	DONNER	ESCAPE	PROGRESS	NORMA

Flowers for Algernon Vocabulary Word List

No.	Word	Clue/Definition
1.	ACCUMULATED	Gathered or piled up
2.	ADMINISTERED	Given out; dispensed
3.	ADMONISH	To reprimand gently but earnestly
4.	AMNESIA	Partial or total loss of memory
5.	APPRENTICE	One who is learning a trade or occupation
6.	BERSERK	Destructively or frenetically violent
7.	COMPLICATED	Not easy to understand or analyze; complex
8.	COMPOSURE	A calm state of mind
9.	CONSCIOUS	Aware
10.	CONSISTENT	Reliable or uniform
11.	CORDIAL	Friendly
12.	COWERS	Cringes in fear
13.	CYNICAL	Expressing scorn and bitter mockery
14.	DEGENERATE	A depraved, corrupt, or vicious person
15.	DEPRAVED	Corrupt; wicked
16.	DESPISING	Disliking intensely
17.	DETERIORATION	A steady lowering of quality
18.	DOCILE	Yielding to supervision or management
19.	ENCOMPASSING	Surrounding
20.	ERRATIC	Irregular; not uniform
21.	EUPHEMISMS	Mild terms used for offensive ones
22.	EXIGENCIES	Urgent requirements; pressing needs
23.	FLAIL	To strike or lash out violently
24.	FUGUES	Amnesiac conditions
25.	FUTILE	Having no useful result
26.	HUNCHES	Assumes a crouched or cramped posture
27.	IMPERCEPTIBLY	Without being seen or noticed
28.	IMPLICATION	Something hinted or suggested
29.	IMPULSE	Sudden wish or urge
30.	INEVITABLE	Impossible to avoid or prevent
31.	INTUITION	Knowing or sensing without rational processes
32.	IRONIC	Contrary to what was expected or intended
33.	ISOLATED	Set apart or cut off from others
34.	JUXTAPOSITION	Placement side by side for comparison
35.	LABYRINTH	A maze
36.	LETHARGY	State of sluggishness or inactivity
37.	LUMINESCENT	Emitting light
38.	MAROONED	Abandoned or isolated with little hope of rescue
39.	MASSIVE	Large
40.	NAIVETE	The state of being unaware of something that most people know; innocence
41.	NUMB	Unresponsive; unfeeling
42.	OBLIGATIONS	Duties or promises
43.	OBSTRUCTION	Something in the way
44.	ORNATELY	Flashy, showy, intricate in style or manner
45.	PARADOXICAL	Seemingly contradictory but possibly true
46.	PATHOLOGY	The scientific study of disease
47.	PECULIAR	Unusual or eccentric; odd
48.	PERMANENT	Unchanging
49.	PHENOMENAL	Extraordinary; outstanding
50.	PLATEAU	A stable or level state

Flowers for Algernon Vocabulary Word List Continued

No. Word	Clue/Definition
51. PLATONIC	Spiritual or ideal, not physical
52. POMPOUS	Arrogant; having excessive self-esteem
53. PRECAUTION	Action taken to prevent possible danger
54. PROCEDURE	Series of steps to accomplish something
55. PROGNOSIS	Prediction of the possible outcome of a disease
56. QUEASY	Causing nausea; sickening
57. RECEDE	To move back or away from
58. SKEPTICAL	Doubtful
59. STUPOR	State of mental numbness
60. SUPERIMPOSED	Placed on or over something else
61. USURPED	Taken over or occupied without right
62. VAGUE	Indistinctly felt, perceived, or understood
63. VALID	True; correct
64. VESTIBULE	Entrance hall
65. WARD	Try to prevent

Copyrighted

Flowers for Algernon Vocabulary Fill In The Blank 1

_____ 1. Taken over or occupied without right

_____ 2. Contrary to what was expected or intended

_____ 3. One who is learning a trade or occupation

_____ 4. Unchanging

_____ 5. To reprimand gently but earnestly

_____ 6. Entrance hall

_____ 7. Placed on or over something else

_____ 8. Amnesiac conditions

_____ 9. Irregular; not uniform

_____ 10. Large

_____ 11. Expressing scorn and bitter mockery

_____ 12. Indistinctly felt, perceived, or understood

_____ 13. A maze

_____ 14. Doubtful

_____ 15. Try to prevent

_____ 16. Duties or promises

_____ 17. Assumes a crouched or cramped posture

_____ 18. Friendly

_____ 19. State of mental numbness

_____ 20. Given out; dispensed

Flowers for Algernon Vocabulary Fill In The Blank 1 Answer Key

USURPED	1. Taken over or occupied without right
IRONIC	2. Contrary to what was expected or intended
APPRENTICE	3. One who is learning a trade or occupation
PERMANENT	4. Unchanging
ADMONISH	5. To reprimand gently but earnestly
VESTIBULE	6. Entrance hall
SUPERIMPOSED	7. Placed on or over something else
FUGUES	8. Amnesiac conditions
ERRATIC	9. Irregular; not uniform
MASSIVE	10. Large
CYNICAL	11. Expressing scorn and bitter mockery
VAGUE	12. Indistinctly felt, perceived, or understood
LABYRINTH	13. A maze
SKEPTICAL	14. Doubtful
WARD	15. Try to prevent
OBLIGATIONS	16. Duties or promises
HUNCHES	17. Assumes a crouched or cramped posture
CORDIAL	18. Friendly
STUPOR	19. State of mental numbness
ADMINISTERED	20. Given out; dispensed

Flowers for Algernon Vocabulary Fill In The Blank 2

_____ 1. Disliking intensely

_____ 2. A maze

_____ 3. Placed on or over something else

_____ 4. State of mental numbness

_____ 5. The state of being unaware of something that most people know; innocence

_____ 6. Unusual or eccentric; odd

_____ 7. Placement side by side for comparison

_____ 8. True; correct

_____ 9. Expressing scorn and bitter mockery

_____ 10. Emitting light

_____ 11. Something in the way

_____ 12. Corrupt; wicked

_____ 13. Urgent requirements; pressing needs

_____ 14. Flashy, showy, intricate in style or manner

_____ 15. To strike or lash out violently

_____ 16. Aware

_____ 17. Sudden wish or urge

_____ 18. Spiritual or ideal, not physical

_____ 19. A depraved, corrupt, or vicious person

_____ 20. Surrounding

Flowers for Algernon Vocabulary Fill In The Blank 2 Answer Key

DESPISING	1. Disliking intensely
LABYRINTH	2. A maze
SUPERIMPOSED	3. Placed on or over something else
STUPOR	4. State of mental numbness
NAIVETE	5. The state of being unaware of something that most people know; innocence
PECULIAR	6. Unusual or eccentric; odd
JUXTAPOSITION	7. Placement side by side for comparison
VALID	8. True; correct
CYNICAL	9. Expressing scorn and bitter mockery
LUMINESCENT	10. Emitting light
OBSTRUCTION	11. Something in the way
DEPRAVED	12. Corrupt; wicked
EXIGENCIES	13. Urgent requirements; pressing needs
ORNATELY	14. Flashy, showy, intricate in style or manner
FLAIL	15. To strike or lash out violently
CONSCIOUS	16. Aware
IMPULSE	17. Sudden wish or urge
PLATONIC	18. Spiritual or ideal, not physical
DEGENERATE	19. A depraved, corrupt, or vicious person
ENCOMPASSING	20. Surrounding

Flowers for Algernon Vocabulary Fill In The Blank 3

_____ 1. One who is learning a trade or occupation

_____ 2. Not easy to understand or analyze; complex

_____ 3. Cringes in fear

_____ 4. Something hinted or suggested

_____ 5. Extraordinary; outstanding

_____ 6. Entrance hall

_____ 7. A maze

_____ 8. Reliable or uniform

_____ 9. A stable or level state

_____ 10. Arrogant; having excessive self-esteem

_____ 11. Having no useful result

_____ 12. Contrary to what was expected or intended

_____ 13. True; correct

_____ 14. Disliking intensely

_____ 15. Prediction of the possible outcome of a disease

_____ 16. Set apart or cut off from others

_____ 17. Unresponsive; unfeeling

_____ 18. Aware

_____ 19. Amnesiac conditions

_____ 20. A depraved, corrupt, or vicious person

Flowers for Algernon Vocabulary Fill In The Blank 3 Answer Key

APPRENTICE	1. One who is learning a trade or occupation
COMPLICATED	2. Not easy to understand or analyze; complex
COWERS	3. Cringes in fear
IMPLICATION	4. Something hinted or suggested
PHENOMENAL	5. Extraordinary; outstanding
VESTIBULE	6. Entrance hall
LABYRINTH	7. A maze
CONSISTENT	8. Reliable or uniform
PLATEAU	9. A stable or level state
POMPOUS	10. Arrogant; having excessive self-esteem
FUTILE	11. Having no useful result
IRONIC	12. Contrary to what was expected or intended
VALID	13. True; correct
DESPISING	14. Disliking intensely
PROGNOSIS	15. Prediction of the possible outcome of a disease
ISOLATED	16. Set apart or cut off from others
NUMB	17. Unresponsive; unfeeling
CONSCIOUS	18. Aware
FUGUES	19. Amnesiac conditions
DEGENERATE	20. A depraved, corrupt, or vicious person

Flowers for Algernon Vocabulary Fill In The Blank 4

_____ 1. Friendly

_____ 2. A maze

_____ 3. State of mental numbness

_____ 4. Placement side by side for comparison

_____ 5. Surrounding

_____ 6. Irregular; not uniform

_____ 7. Unusual or eccentric; odd

_____ 8. Gathered or piled up

_____ 9. Given out; dispensed

_____ 10. Something hinted or suggested

_____ 11. Abandoned or isolated with little hope of rescue

_____ 12. Emitting light

_____ 13. Not easy to understand or analyze; complex

_____ 14. Destructively or frenetically violent

_____ 15. Doubtful

_____ 16. One who is learning a trade or occupation

_____ 17. Without being seen or noticed

_____ 18. Causing nausea; sickening

_____ 19. State of sluggishness or inactivity

_____ 20. Having no useful result

Flowers for Algernon Vocabulary Fill In The Blank 4 Answer Key

CORDIAL	1. Friendly
LABYRINTH	2. A maze
STUPOR	3. State of mental numbness
JUXTAPOSITION	4. Placement side by side for comparison
ENCOMPASSING	5. Surrounding
ERRATIC	6. Irregular; not uniform
PECULIAR	7. Unusual or eccentric; odd
ACCUMULATED	8. Gathered or piled up
ADMINISTERED	9. Given out; dispensed
IMPLICATION	10. Something hinted or suggested
MAROONED	11. Abandoned or isolated with little hope of rescue
LUMINESCENT	12. Emitting light
COMPLICATED	13. Not easy to understand or analyze; complex
BERSERK	14. Destructively or frenetically violent
SKEPTICAL	15. Doubtful
APPRENTICE	16. One who is learning a trade or occupation
IMPERCEPTIBLY	17. Without being seen or noticed
QUEASY	18. Causing nausea; sickening
LETHARGY	19. State of sluggishness or inactivity
FUTILE	20. Having no useful result

Flowers for Algernon Vocabulary Matching 1

___ 1. USURPED   A. Urgent requirements; pressing needs
___ 2. MAROONED   B. Corrupt; wicked
___ 3. CORDIAL   C. Abandoned or isolated with little hope of rescue
___ 4. ENCOMPASSING   D. Surrounding
___ 5. FLAIL   E. Friendly
___ 6. QUEASY   F. A stable or level state
___ 7. LETHARGY   G. Placed on or over something else
___ 8. SUPERIMPOSED   H. Causing nausea; sickening
___ 9. LABYRINTH   I. Knowing or sensing without rational processes
___10. DETERIORATION   J. A maze
___11. ISOLATED   K. To strike or lash out violently
___12. PLATEAU   L. Having no useful result
___13. RECEDE   M. Extraordinary; outstanding
___14. ERRATIC   N. Set apart or cut off from others
___15. VALID   O. Contrary to what was expected or intended
___16. IRONIC   P. To move back or away from
___17. INTUITION   Q. Gathered or piled up
___18. EXIGENCIES   R. Series of steps to accomplish something
___19. PHENOMENAL   S. True; correct
___20. PROCEDURE   T. State of sluggishness or inactivity
___21. ACCUMULATED   U. Disliking intensely
___22. DESPISING   V. Prediction of the possible outcome of a disease
___23. DEPRAVED   W. Taken over or occupied without right
___24. FUTILE   X. Irregular; not uniform
___25. PROGNOSIS   Y. A steady lowering of quality

Flowers for Algernon Vocabulary Matching 1 Answer Key

W - 1.	USURPED	A.	Urgent requirements; pressing needs
C - 2.	MAROONED	B.	Corrupt; wicked
E - 3.	CORDIAL	C.	Abandoned or isolated with little hope of rescue
D - 4.	ENCOMPASSING	D.	Surrounding
K - 5.	FLAIL	E.	Friendly
H - 6.	QUEASY	F.	A stable or level state
T - 7.	LETHARGY	G.	Placed on or over something else
G - 8.	SUPERIMPOSED	H.	Causing nausea; sickening
J - 9.	LABYRINTH	I.	Knowing or sensing without rational processes
Y - 10.	DETERIORATION	J.	A maze
N - 11.	ISOLATED	K.	To strike or lash out violently
F - 12.	PLATEAU	L.	Having no useful result
P - 13.	RECEDE	M.	Extraordinary; outstanding
X - 14.	ERRATIC	N.	Set apart or cut off from others
S - 15.	VALID	O.	Contrary to what was expected or intended
O - 16.	IRONIC	P.	To move back or away from
I - 17.	INTUITION	Q.	Gathered or piled up
A - 18.	EXIGENCIES	R.	Series of steps to accomplish something
M - 19.	PHENOMENAL	S.	True; correct
R - 20.	PROCEDURE	T.	State of sluggishness or inactivity
Q - 21.	ACCUMULATED	U.	Disliking intensely
U - 22.	DESPISING	V.	Prediction of the possible outcome of a disease
B - 23.	DEPRAVED	W.	Taken over or occupied without right
L - 24.	FUTILE	X.	Irregular; not uniform
V - 25.	PROGNOSIS	Y.	A steady lowering of quality

Flowers for Algernon Vocabulary Matching 2

___ 1. DESPISING   A. Something hinted or suggested
___ 2. RECEDE   B. Something in the way
___ 3. VALID   C. Cringes in fear
___ 4. FUTILE   D. Entrance hall
___ 5. IMPLICATION   E. Indistinctly felt, perceived, or understood
___ 6. CYNICAL   F. To move back or away from
___ 7. SUPERIMPOSED   G. Corrupt; wicked
___ 8. INTUITION   H. Without being seen or noticed
___ 9. ENCOMPASSING   I. Not easy to understand or analyze; complex
___ 10. ERRATIC   J. Irregular; not uniform
___ 11. EXIGENCIES   K. One who is learning a trade or occupation
___ 12. HUNCHES   L. Mild terms used for offensive ones
___ 13. VESTIBULE   M. True; correct
___ 14. COWERS   N. Aware
___ 15. COMPLICATED   O. Knowing or sensing without rational processes
___ 16. IMPERCEPTIBLY   P. Arrogant; having excessive self-esteem
___ 17. VAGUE   Q. Having no useful result
___ 18. POMPOUS   R. Expressing scorn and bitter mockery
___ 19. CONSCIOUS   S. Disliking intensely
___ 20. APPRENTICE   T. Given out; dispensed
___ 21. EUPHEMISMS   U. Surrounding
___ 22. ADMINISTERED   V. Urgent requirements; pressing needs
___ 23. PATHOLOGY   W. Placed on or over something else
___ 24. OBSTRUCTION   X. Assumes a crouched or cramped posture
___ 25. DEPRAVED   Y. The scientific study of disease

Flowers for Algernon Vocabulary Matching 2 Answer Key

S - 1.	DESPISING	A. Something hinted or suggested
F - 2.	RECEDE	B. Something in the way
M - 3.	VALID	C. Cringes in fear
Q - 4.	FUTILE	D. Entrance hall
A - 5.	IMPLICATION	E. Indistinctly felt, perceived, or understood
R - 6.	CYNICAL	F. To move back or away from
W - 7.	SUPERIMPOSED	G. Corrupt; wicked
O - 8.	INTUITION	H. Without being seen or noticed
U - 9.	ENCOMPASSING	I. Not easy to understand or analyze; complex
J - 10.	ERRATIC	J. Irregular; not uniform
V - 11.	EXIGENCIES	K. One who is learning a trade or occupation
X - 12.	HUNCHES	L. Mild terms used for offensive ones
D - 13.	VESTIBULE	M. True; correct
C - 14.	COWERS	N. Aware
I - 15.	COMPLICATED	O. Knowing or sensing without rational processes
H - 16.	IMPERCEPTIBLY	P. Arrogant; having excessive self-esteem
E - 17.	VAGUE	Q. Having no useful result
P - 18.	POMPOUS	R. Expressing scorn and bitter mockery
N - 19.	CONSCIOUS	S. Disliking intensely
K - 20.	APPRENTICE	T. Given out; dispensed
L - 21.	EUPHEMISMS	U. Surrounding
T - 22.	ADMINISTERED	V. Urgent requirements; pressing needs
Y - 23.	PATHOLOGY	W. Placed on or over something else
B - 24.	OBSTRUCTION	X. Assumes a crouched or cramped posture
G - 25.	DEPRAVED	Y. The scientific study of disease

Flowers for Algernon Vocabulary Matching 3

___ 1. LETHARGY A. Try to prevent
___ 2. IMPERCEPTIBLY B. A calm state of mind
___ 3. WARD C. Doubtful
___ 4. OBSTRUCTION D. Large
___ 5. PARADOXICAL E. Unresponsive; unfeeling
___ 6. ERRATIC F. Given out; dispensed
___ 7. PERMANENT G. Extraordinary; outstanding
___ 8. ISOLATED H. Something in the way
___ 9. VESTIBULE I. Without being seen or noticed
___10. MASSIVE J. State of sluggishness or inactivity
___11. COMPOSURE K. Gathered or piled up
___12. USURPED L. Unchanging
___13. BERSERK M. Seemingly contradictory but possibly true
___14. AMNESIA N. Partial or total loss of memory
___15. ADMINISTERED O. Yielding to supervision or management
___16. ACCUMULATED P. Taken over or occupied without right
___17. PRECAUTION Q. Placed on or over something else
___18. EUPHEMISMS R. A depraved, corrupt, or vicious person
___19. PROCEDURE S. Set apart or cut off from others
___20. DOCILE T. Entrance hall
___21. SKEPTICAL U. Action taken to prevent possible danger
___22. PHENOMENAL V. Irregular; not uniform
___23. SUPERIMPOSED W. Mild terms used for offensive ones
___24. NUMB X. Series of steps to accomplish something
___25. DEGENERATE Y. Destructively or frenetically violent

Flowers for Algernon Vocabulary Matching 3 Answer Key

J -	1. LETHARGY	A.	Try to prevent
I -	2. IMPERCEPTIBLY	B.	A calm state of mind
A -	3. WARD	C.	Doubtful
H -	4. OBSTRUCTION	D.	Large
M -	5. PARADOXICAL	E.	Unresponsive; unfeeling
V -	6. ERRATIC	F.	Given out; dispensed
L -	7. PERMANENT	G.	Extraordinary; outstanding
S -	8. ISOLATED	H.	Something in the way
T -	9. VESTIBULE	I.	Without being seen or noticed
D -	10. MASSIVE	J.	State of sluggishness or inactivity
B -	11. COMPOSURE	K.	Gathered or piled up
P -	12. USURPED	L.	Unchanging
Y -	13. BERSERK	M.	Seemingly contradictory but possibly true
N -	14. AMNESIA	N.	Partial or total loss of memory
F -	15. ADMINISTERED	O.	Yielding to supervision or management
K -	16. ACCUMULATED	P.	Taken over or occupied without right
U -	17. PRECAUTION	Q.	Placed on or over something else
W -	18. EUPHEMISMS	R.	A depraved, corrupt, or vicious person
X -	19. PROCEDURE	S.	Set apart or cut off from others
O -	20. DOCILE	T.	Entrance hall
C -	21. SKEPTICAL	U.	Action taken to prevent possible danger
G -	22. PHENOMENAL	V.	Irregular; not uniform
Q -	23. SUPERIMPOSED	W.	Mild terms used for offensive ones
E -	24. NUMB	X.	Series of steps to accomplish something
R -	25. DEGENERATE	Y.	Destructively or frenetically violent

Flowers for Algernon Vocabulary Matching 4

___ 1. ORNATELY A. Indistinctly felt, perceived, or understood
___ 2. IMPERCEPTIBLY B. Placement side by side for comparison
___ 3. IMPULSE C. Amnesiac conditions
___ 4. DEGENERATE D. Cringes in fear
___ 5. COMPLICATED E. Sudden wish or urge
___ 6. LETHARGY F. Something in the way
___ 7. AMNESIA G. State of sluggishness or inactivity
___ 8. ERRATIC H. Irregular; not uniform
___ 9. NAIVETE I. Not easy to understand or analyze; complex
___10. RECEDE J. Flashy, showy, intricate in style or manner
___11. CONSCIOUS K. Set apart or cut off from others
___12. MAROONED L. To move back or away from
___13. PERMANENT M. Contrary to what was expected or intended
___14. COWERS N. Friendly
___15. VAGUE O. Partial or total loss of memory
___16. EUPHEMISMS P. Expressing scorn and bitter mockery
___17. POMPOUS Q. A depraved, corrupt, or vicious person
___18. CORDIAL R. Aware
___19. CYNICAL S. Without being seen or noticed
___20. JUXTAPOSITION T. Arrogant; having excessive self-esteem
___21. OBSTRUCTION U. Mild terms used for offensive ones
___22. EXIGENCIES V. Unchanging
___23. ISOLATED W. Abandoned or isolated with little hope of rescue
___24. FUGUES X. The state of being unaware of something that most people know; innocence
___25. IRONIC Y. Urgent requirements; pressing needs

Flowers for Algernon Vocabulary Matching 4

J - 1. ORNATELY	A.	Indistinctly felt, perceived, or understood
S - 2. IMPERCEPTIBLY	B.	Placement side by side for comparison
E - 3. IMPULSE	C.	Amnesiac conditions
Q - 4. DEGENERATE	D.	Cringes in fear
I - 5. COMPLICATED	E.	Sudden wish or urge
G - 6. LETHARGY	F.	Something in the way
O - 7. AMNESIA	G.	State of sluggishness or inactivity
H - 8. ERRATIC	H.	Irregular; not uniform
X - 9. NAIVETE	I.	Not easy to understand or analyze; complex
L - 10. RECEDE	J.	Flashy, showy, intricate in style or manner
R - 11. CONSCIOUS	K.	Set apart or cut off from others
W - 12. MAROONED	L.	To move back or away from
V - 13. PERMANENT	M.	Contrary to what was expected or intended
D - 14. COWERS	N.	Friendly
A - 15. VAGUE	O.	Partial or total loss of memory
U - 16. EUPHEMISMS	P.	Expressing scorn and bitter mockery
T - 17. POMPOUS	Q.	A depraved, corrupt, or vicious person
N - 18. CORDIAL	R.	Aware
P - 19. CYNICAL	S.	Without being seen or noticed
B - 20. JUXTAPOSITION	T.	Arrogant; having excessive self-esteem
F - 21. OBSTRUCTION	U.	Mild terms used for offensive ones
Y - 22. EXIGENCIES	V.	Unchanging
K - 23. ISOLATED	W.	Abandoned or isolated with little hope of rescue
C - 24. FUGUES	X.	The state of being unaware of something that most people know; innocence
M - 25. IRONIC	Y.	Urgent requirements; pressing needs

Flowers for Algernon Vocabulary Magic Squares 1

Match the definition with the vocabulary word. Put your answers in the magic squares below. When your answers are correct, all columns and rows will add to the same number.

A. PROGNOSIS
B. STUPOR
C. ISOLATED
D. CORDIAL
E. DETERIORATION
F. ADMINISTERED
G. VAGUE
H. WARD
I. CONSISTENT
J. INTUITION
K. EXIGENCIES
L. IMPLICATION
M. ORNATELY
N. CONSCIOUS
O. PECULIAR
P. EUPHEMISMS

1. Unusual or eccentric; odd
2. Knowing or sensing without rational processes
3. Try to prevent
4. Prediction of the possible outcome of a disease
5. Friendly
6. A steady lowering of quality
7. Urgent requirements; pressing needs
8. Aware
9. Given out; dispensed
10. Set apart or cut off from others
11. Flashy, showy, intricate in style or manner
12. Something hinted or suggested
13. Reliable or uniform
14. Mild terms used for offensive ones
15. State of mental numbness
16. Indistinctly felt, perceived, or understood

A=	B=	C=	D=
E=	F=	G=	H=
I=	J=	K=	L=
M=	N=	O=	P=

Flowers for Algernon Vocabulary Magic Squares 1 Answer Key

Match the definition with the vocabulary word. Put your answers in the magic squares below. When your answers are correct, all columns and rows will add to the same number.

A. PROGNOSIS
B. STUPOR
C. ISOLATED
D. CORDIAL
E. DETERIORATION
F. ADMINISTERED
G. VAGUE
H. WARD
I. CONSISTENT
J. INTUITION
K. EXIGENCIES
L. IMPLICATION
M. ORNATELY
N. CONSCIOUS
O. PECULIAR
P. EUPHEMISMS

1. Unusual or eccentric; odd
2. Knowing or sensing without rational processes
3. Try to prevent
4. Prediction of the possible outcome of a disease
5. Friendly
6. A steady lowering of quality
7. Urgent requirements; pressing needs
8. Aware
9. Given out; dispensed
10. Set apart or cut off from others
11. Flashy, showy, intricate in style or manner
12. Something hinted or suggested
13. Reliable or uniform
14. Mild terms used for offensive ones
15. State of mental numbness
16. Indistinctly felt, perceived, or understood

A=4	B=15	C=10	D=5
E=6	F=9	G=16	H=3
I=13	J=2	K=7	L=12
M=11	N=8	O=1	P=14

Flowers for Algernon Vocabulary Magic Squares 2

Match the definition with the vocabulary word. Put your answers in the magic squares below. When your answers are correct, all columns and rows will add to the same number.

A. EUPHEMISMS   E. JUXTAPOSITION   I. DEGENERATE   M. VALID
B. PERMANENT   F. INEVITABLE   J. PRECAUTION   N. PHENOMENAL
C. ADMINISTERED   G. LUMINESCENT   K. PECULIAR   O. IRONIC
D. LETHARGY   H. POMPOUS   L. BERSERK   P. COMPOSURE

1. Arrogant; having excessive self-esteem
2. True; correct
3. Unchanging
4. Unusual or eccentric; odd
5. Action taken to prevent possible danger
6. Given out; dispensed
7. A calm state of mind
8. Placement side by side for comparison
9. Contrary to what was expected or intended
10. Impossible to avoid or prevent
11. A depraved, corrupt, or vicious person
12. State of sluggishness or inactivity
13. Mild terms used for offensive ones
14. Destructively or frenetically violent
15. Emitting light
16. Extraordinary; outstanding

A=	B=	C=	D=
E=	F=	G=	H=
I=	J=	K=	L=
M=	N=	O=	P=

Flowers for Algernon Vocabulary Magic Squares 2 Answer Key

Match the definition with the vocabulary word. Put your answers in the magic squares below. When your answers are correct, all columns and rows will add to the same number.

A. EUPHEMISMS
B. PERMANENT
C. ADMINISTERED
D. LETHARGY
E. JUXTAPOSITION
F. INEVITABLE
G. LUMINESCENT
H. POMPOUS
I. DEGENERATE
J. PRECAUTION
K. PECULIAR
L. BERSERK
M. VALID
N. PHENOMENAL
O. IRONIC
P. COMPOSURE

1. Arrogant; having excessive self-esteem
2. True; correct
3. Unchanging
4. Unusual or eccentric; odd
5. Action taken to prevent possible danger
6. Given out; dispensed
7. A calm state of mind
8. Placement side by side for comparison
9. Contrary to what was expected or intended
10. Impossible to avoid or prevent
11. A depraved, corrupt, or vicious person
12. State of sluggishness or inactivity
13. Mild terms used for offensive ones
14. Destructively or frenetically violent
15. Emitting light
16. Extraordinary; outstanding

A=13	B=3	C=6	D=12
E=8	F=10	G=15	H=1
I=11	J=5	K=4	L=14
M=2	N=16	O=9	P=7

Flowers for Algernon Vocabulary Magic Squares 3

Match the definition with the vocabulary word. Put your answers in the magic squares below. When your answers are correct, all columns and rows will add to the same number.

A. AMNESIA
B. QUEASY
C. MASSIVE
D. HUNCHES
E. EUPHEMISMS
F. PLATEAU
G. IMPULSE
H. MAROONED
I. DESPISING
J. IMPERCEPTIBLY
K. CONSCIOUS
L. ADMONISH
M. APPRENTICE
N. NAIVETE
O. PATHOLOGY
P. IMPLICATION

1. A stable or level state
2. Disliking intensely
3. The scientific study of disease
4. Assumes a crouched or cramped posture
5. One who is learning a trade or occupation
6. Causing nausea; sickening
7. Abandoned or isolated with little hope of rescue
8. Aware
9. Large
10. Something hinted or suggested
11. Without being seen or noticed
12. Mild terms used for offensive ones
13. To reprimand gently but earnestly
14. Sudden wish or urge
15. Partial or total loss of memory
16. The state of being unaware of something that most people know; innocence innocence

A=	B=	C=	D=
E=	F=	G=	H=
I=	J=	K=	L=
M=	N=	O=	P=

Flowers for Algernon Vocabulary Magic Squares 3 Answer Key

Match the definition with the vocabulary word. Put your answers in the magic squares below. When your answers are correct, all columns and rows will add to the same number.

A. AMNESIA	E. EUPHEMISMS	I. DESPISING	M. APPRENTICE
B. QUEASY	F. PLATEAU	J. IMPERCEPTIBLY	N. NAIVETE
C. MASSIVE	G. IMPULSE	K. CONSCIOUS	O. PATHOLOGY
D. HUNCHES	H. MAROONED	L. ADMONISH	P. IMPLICATION

1. A stable or level state
2. Disliking intensely
3. The scientific study of disease
4. Assumes a crouched or cramped posture
5. One who is learning a trade or occupation
6. Causing nausea; sickening
7. Abandoned or isolated with little hope of rescue
8. Aware
9. Large
10. Something hinted or suggested
11. Without being seen or noticed
12. Mild terms used for offensive ones
13. To reprimand gently but earnestly
14. Sudden wish or urge
15. Partial or total loss of memory
16. The state of being unaware of something that most people know; innocence innocence

A=15	B=6	C=9	D=4
E=12	F=1	G=14	H=7
I=2	J=11	K=8	L=13
M=5	N=16	O=3	P=10

Flowers For Algernon Vocabulary Magic Squares 4

A. HUNCHES
B. VALID
C. LUMINESCENT
D. ISOLATED
E. LETHARGY
F. PERMANENT
G. PROCEDURE
H. STUPOR
I. DESPISING
J. AMNESIA
K. ACCUMULATED
L. VAGUE
M. ERRATIC
N. RECEDE
O. OBLIGATIONS
P. FLAIL

1. Irregular; not uniform
2. Unchanging
3. State of mental numbness
4. Duties or promises
5. Indistinctly felt, perceived, or understood
6. Emitting light
7. Assumes a crouched or cramped posture
8. Partial or total loss of memory
9. Gathered or piled up
10. Set apart or cut off from others
11. True; correct
12. Disliking intensely
13. To move back or away from
14. State of sluggishness or inactivity
15. Series of steps to accomplish something
16. To strike or lash out violently

A=	B=	C=	D=
E=	F=	G=	H=
I=	J=	K=	L=
M=	N=	O=	P=

Flowers For Algernon Vocabulary Magic Squares 4 Answer Key

A. HUNCHES
B. VALID
C. LUMINESCENT
D. ISOLATED
E. LETHARGY
F. PERMANENT
G. PROCEDURE
H. STUPOR
I. DESPISING
J. AMNESIA
K. ACCUMULATED
L. VAGUE
M. ERRATIC
N. RECEDE
O. OBLIGATIONS
P. FLAIL

1. Irregular; not uniform
2. Unchanging
3. State of mental numbness
4. Duties or promises
5. Indistinctly felt, perceived, or understood
6. Emitting light
7. Assumes a crouched or cramped posture
8. Partial or total loss of memory
9. Gathered or piled up
10. Set apart or cut off from others
11. True; correct
12. Disliking intensely
13. To move back or away from
14. State of sluggishness or inactivity
15. Series of steps to accomplish something
16. To strike or lash out violently

A=7	B=11	C=6	D=10
E=14	F=2	G=15	H=3
I=12	J=8	K=9	L=5
M=1	N=13	O=4	P=16

Flowers For Algernon Vocabulary Word Search 1

```
P L A T E A U P R O G N O S I S E W C
E A C M Q U E A S Y U K U M S E R A O
Q U T U N G Z M P M Q O Y A O U R R W
M X P H S E M K B R P Y R S L G A D E
L A D H O U S Q B M P J A S A U T I R
S J R B E L R I O K A X I I T F I N S
R K Z O N M O P A V R Y L V E G C T S
D D E Y O I I G E V A G U E D C M U N
S E Q P K N M S Y D D B C R D R C I O
A G P F T C E P M K O J E Y L I N T I
D E D R I I F D L S X P P C N E W I T
M N S N A W C U M I I R L O V I E O A
O E O K D V R A T Z C S T I Y S C N G
N R B V O E E K L I A A T J L Y S A I
I A K N C O R D I A L A T U F L A I L
S T G E I Z L I W P B E P I P H Z V B
H E D Y L D P L Y L N M Z P O O J E O
B E R S E R K A E P I P B N G N R T S
H U N C H E S V S E I C N E G I X E J
```

A depraved, corrupt, or vicious person (10)
A stable or level state (7)
Abandoned or isolated with little hope of rescue (8)
Amnesiac conditions (6)
Arrogant; having excessive self-esteem (7)
Assumes a crouched or cramped posture (7)
Causing nausea; sickening (6)
Contrary to what was expected or intended (6)
Corrupt; wicked (8)
Cringes in fear (6)
Destructively or frenetically violent (7)
Doubtful (9)
Duties or promises (11)
Expressing scorn and bitter mockery (7)
Friendly (7)
Having no useful result (6)
Impossible to avoid or prevent (10)
Indistinctly felt, perceived, or understood (5)
Irregular; not uniform (7)
Knowing or sensing without rational processes (9)
Large (7)

Mild terms used for offensive ones (10)
Partial or total loss of memory (7)
Prediction of the possible outcome of a disease (9)
Seemingly contradictory but possibly true (11)
Set apart or cut off from others (8)
Something hinted or suggested (11)
Spiritual or ideal, not physical (8)
State of mental numbness (6)
Sudden wish or urge (7)
Taken over or occupied without right (7)
The scientific study of disease (9)
The state of being unaware of something that most people know; innocence (7)
To move back or away from (6)
To reprimand gently but earnestly (8)
To strike or lash out violently (5)
True; correct (5)
Try to prevent (4)
Unresponsive; unfeeling (4)
Unusual or eccentric; odd (8)
Urgent requirements; pressing needs (10)
Yielding to supervision or management (6)

Flowers For Algernon Vocabulary Word Search 1 Answer Key

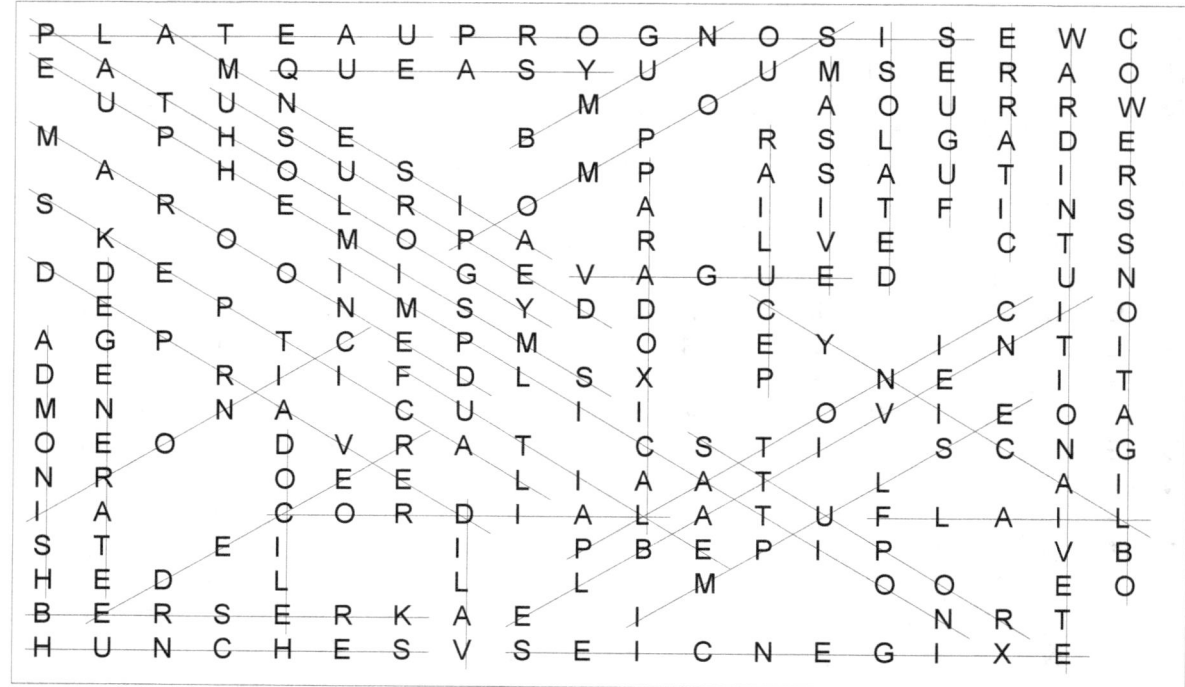

A depraved, corrupt, or vicious person (10)
A stable or level state (7)
Abandoned or isolated with little hope of rescue (8)
Amnesiac conditions (6)
Arrogant; having excessive self-esteem (7)
Assumes a crouched or cramped posture (7)
Causing nausea; sickening (6)
Contrary to what was expected or intended (6)
Corrupt; wicked (8)
Cringes in fear (6)
Destructively or frenetically violent (7)
Doubtful (9)
Duties or promises (11)
Expressing scorn and bitter mockery (7)
Friendly (7)
Having no useful result (6)
Impossible to avoid or prevent (10)
Indistinctly felt, perceived, or understood (5)
Irregular; not uniform (7)
Knowing or sensing without rational processes (9)
Large (7)

Mild terms used for offensive ones (10)
Partial or total loss of memory (7)
Prediction of the possible outcome of a disease (9)
Seemingly contradictory but possibly true (11)
Set apart or cut off from others (8)
Something hinted or suggested (11)
Spiritual or ideal, not physical (8)
State of mental numbness (6)
Sudden wish or urge (7)
Taken over or occupied without right (7)
The scientific study of disease (9)
The state of being unaware of something that most people know; innocence (7)
To move back or away from (6)
To reprimand gently but earnestly (8)
To strike or lash out violently (5)
True; correct (5)
Try to prevent (4)
Unresponsive; unfeeling (4)
Unusual or eccentric; odd (8)
Urgent requirements; pressing needs (10)
Yielding to supervision or management (6)

Flowers For Algernon Vocabulary Word Search 2

```
I M P E R C E P T I B L Y G K V M A D
P S M D X C M L L N V W R R P F A M E
A I O Z G I R A Y D S W E N R A S N T
T S O L L N G W R W B S C F O P S E E
H O U R A O R E L O R K E G C P I S R
O N S K N T F Q N E O T D D E R V I I
L G U Z B A E T B C A N E Y D E E A O
O O R L N L T D Y R I Z E V U N E P R
G R P A K P C E E D N E E D R T Y Y A
Y P E C L R S N L Q O S S J E I G V T
W C D I H N E F Z Y T C D V Y C R A I
L A E X Y G P U M I H P I B S E A G O
A C R O E R N G B Z U A E L A N H U N
C O R D I A L U M I N E S C E N T E W
I W A A X Q L E M V C L L I U B E P B
N E T R B E Y S X B H I U N Q L L Q K
Y R I A W F X B Z L E T P O R F I N C
C S C P L A T E A U S U M R D I L A V
F L A I L S T U P O R F I I Q T X W R
```

A depraved, corrupt, or vicious person (10)
A stable or level state (7)
A steady lowering of quality (13)
Abandoned or isolated with little hope of rescue (8)
Amnesiac conditions (6)
Assumes a crouched or cramped posture (7)
Causing nausea; sickening (6)
Contrary to what was expected or intended (6)
Cringes in fear (6)
Destructively or frenetically violent (7)
Emitting light (11)
Entrance hall (9)
Expressing scorn and bitter mockery (7)
Flashy, showy, intricate in style or manner (8)
Friendly (7)
Having no useful result (6)
Indistinctly felt, perceived, or understood (5)
Irregular; not uniform (7)
Large (7)
One who is learning a trade or occupation (10)
Partial or total loss of memory (7)
Prediction of the possible outcome of a disease (9)
Seemingly contradictory but possibly true (11)
Series of steps to accomplish something (9)
Set apart or cut off from others (8)
Spiritual or ideal, not physical (8)
State of mental numbness (6)
State of sluggishness or inactivity (8)
Sudden wish or urge (7)
Taken over or occupied without right (7)
The scientific study of disease (9)
The state of being unaware of something that most people know; innocence (7)
To move back or away from (6)
To strike or lash out violently (5)
True; correct (5)
Try to prevent (4)
Unresponsive; unfeeling (4)
Unusual or eccentric; odd (8)
Urgent requirements; pressing needs (10)
Without being seen or noticed (13)
Yielding to supervision or management (6)

Flowers For Algernon Vocabulary Word Search 2 Answer Key

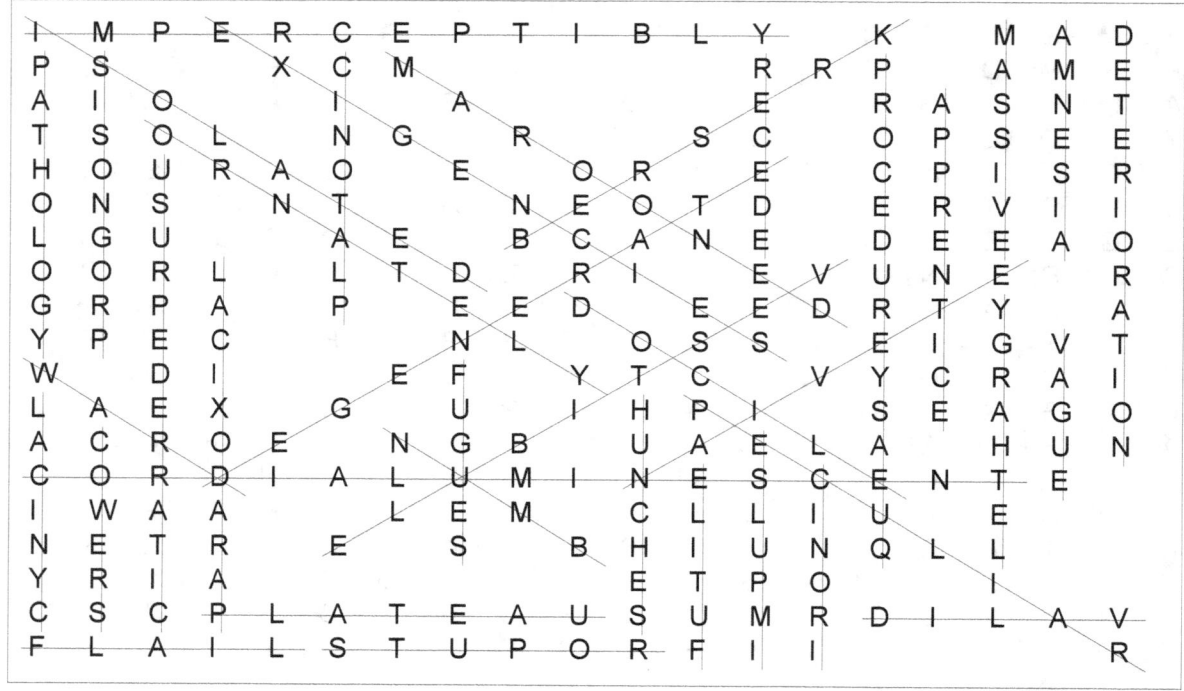

A depraved, corrupt, or vicious person (10)
A stable or level state (7)
A steady lowering of quality (13)
Abandoned or isolated with little hope of rescue (8)
Amnesiac conditions (6)
Assumes a crouched or cramped posture (7)
Causing nausea; sickening (6)
Contrary to what was expected or intended (6)
Cringes in fear (6)
Destructively or frenetically violent (7)
Emitting light (11)
Entrance hall (9)
Expressing scorn and bitter mockery (7)
Flashy, showy, intricate in style or manner (8)
Friendly (7)
Having no useful result (6)
Indistinctly felt, perceived, or understood (5)
Irregular; not uniform (7)
Large (7)
One who is learning a trade or occupation (10)

Partial or total loss of memory (7)
Prediction of the possible outcome of a disease (9)
Seemingly contradictory but possibly true (11)
Series of steps to accomplish something (9)
Set apart or cut off from others (8)
Spiritual or ideal, not physical (8)
State of mental numbness (6)
State of sluggishness or inactivity (8)
Sudden wish or urge (7)
Taken over or occupied without right (7)
The scientific study of disease (9)
The state of being unaware of something that most people know; innocence (7)
To move back or away from (6)
To strike or lash out violently (5)
True; correct (5)
Try to prevent (4)
Unresponsive; unfeeling (4)
Unusual or eccentric; odd (8)
Urgent requirements; pressing needs (10)
Without being seen or noticed (13)
Yielding to supervision or management (6)

Flowers For Algernon Vocabulary Word Search 3

```
L E T H A R G Y M A S S I V E A C I N
P U N Y U S R P E D R J R X M O N O
R G N G R N M J P Y O F R M I N R I
O A N O A J C T G N F A Q A G E D T
G V L L I T X H I Z T P D R E S I C
N C V O L S S C E I W O X O N I I U
O O E H U U W V C S S M T O C A I R
S W S T C W M Y B K M P N N I C O T
I E T A E V C I E E W O A E E S N S
S R I P P Y S P N X R U I D S H E B
K S B E Z G T N F E Z S V W X T C O
W P U R F I M P U L S E E A A F O A
R J L M C D J N G Q V C T R D L N D
E K E A C C U M U L A T E D K A S M
C F L N T M M E E Z L N D N T I C O
E H P E B O A W S L E B L E T L I N
D X G N B S N M T G C R L G H S O I
E V Q T Y K Q I E D Q Y L R O P U S
I S O L A T E D C F U T I L E G S W H
```

ACCUMULATED	HUNCHES	PECULIAR
ADMONISH	IMPULSE	PERMANENT
AMNESIA	INTUITION	PLATONIC
BERSERK	IRONIC	POMPOUS
CONSCIOUS	ISOLATED	PROGNOSIS
CORDIAL	LETHARGY	QUEASY
COWERS	LUMINESCENT	RECEDE
DEGENERATE	MAROONED	SKEPTICAL
DOCILE	MASSIVE	STUPOR
ERRATIC	NAIVETE	USURPED
EXIGENCIES	NUMB	VAGUE
FLAIL	OBSTRUCTION	VALID
FUGUES	ORNATELY	VESTIBULE
FUTILE	PATHOLOGY	WARD

Flowers For Algernon Vocabulary Word Search 3 Answer Key

- ACCUMULATED
- ADMONISH
- AMNESIA
- BERSERK
- CONSCIOUS
- CORDIAL
- COWERS
- DEGENERATE
- DOCILE
- ERRATIC
- EXIGENCIES
- FLAIL
- FUGUES
- FUTILE
- HUNCHES
- IMPULSE
- INTUITION
- IRONIC
- ISOLATED
- LETHARGY
- LUMINESCENT
- MAROONED
- MASSIVE
- NAIVETE
- NUMB
- OBSTRUCTION
- ORNATELY
- PATHOLOGY
- PECULIAR
- PERMANENT
- PLATONIC
- POMPOUS
- PROGNOSIS
- QUEASY
- RECEDE
- SKEPTICAL
- STUPOR
- USURPED
- VAGUE
- VALID
- VESTIBULE
- WARD

Flowers For Algernon Vocabulary Word Search 4

```
I N E V I T A B L E G P O M P O U S C
D E V I S S A M N O I T C U R T S B O
O X C Y N I C A L F X Q I R O N Y X N
C I T A R R E J D P L U X R G N Y P S
I G H N P D D E Y L E T A N R O S I
L E Z C J L W J T P P A M Z O E M W S
E N H Y S A C Y A Z X S D P S S V D T
T C F P A T H O L O G Y V D I L A V E
M I Z U D O N A O E P V T M S U G A N
B E B X T N C A S N T L E B D P U P T
S S F L A I L B I F X H A F T M E P D
S D C R T C L M J V P T A L I F R E
W L V P E D F E A U E U H R E U Z N P
F A E V Z C O W E R S T S U G A S N R
T K R A I S E N M A O Q E U N Y U T A
S S L D N V C D U W P O E Q R C H I V
P E C U L I A R E M Y S N Y Z P H C E
I M P E R C E P T I B L Y E T X E D
A D M O N I S H S T U P O R D C H D S
```

ADMONISH	HUNCHES	PECULIAR
AMNESIA	IMPERCEPTIBLY	PLATEAU
APPRENTICE	IMPULSE	PLATONIC
CONSISTENT	INEVITABLE	POMPOUS
COWERS	IRONIC	PROGNOSIS
CYNICAL	ISOLATED	QUEASY
DEPRAVED	LETHARGY	RECEDE
DOCILE	MAROONED	SKEPTICAL
ERRATIC	MASSIVE	STUPOR
EUPHEMISMS	NAIVETE	USURPED
EXIGENCIES	NUMB	VAGUE
FLAIL	OBSTRUCTION	VALID
FUGUES	ORNATELY	WARD
FUTILE	PATHOLOGY	

Flowers For Algernon Vocabulary Word Search 4 Answer Key

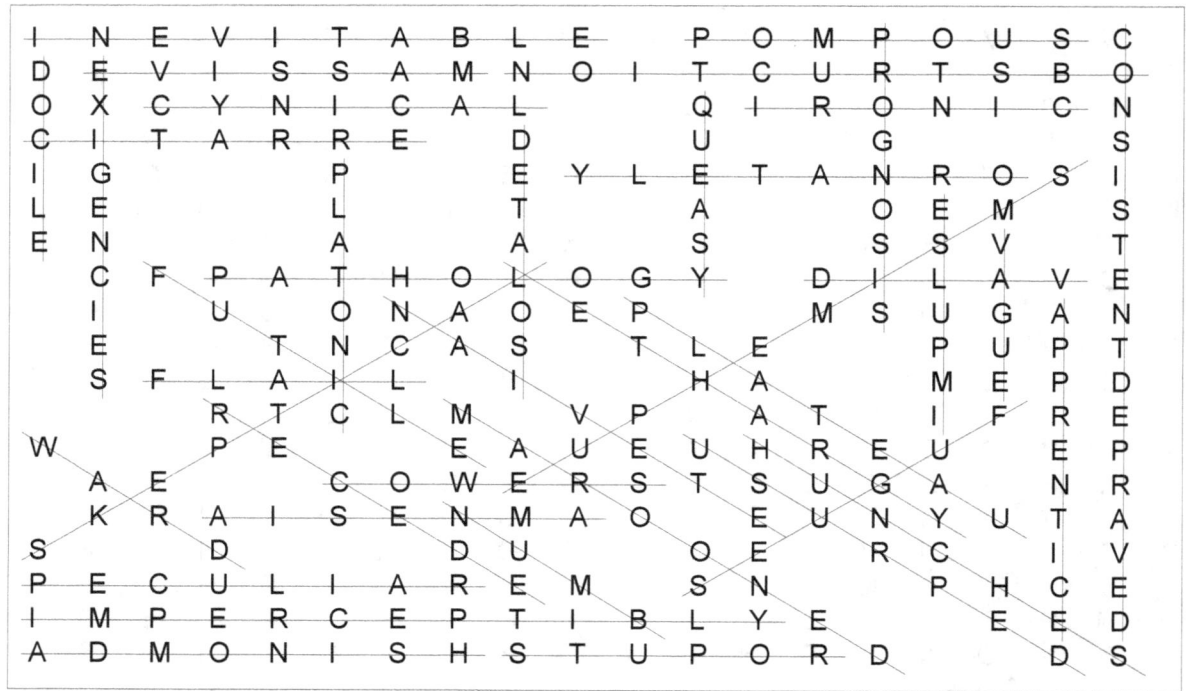

- ADMONISH
- AMNESIA
- APPRENTICE
- CONSISTENT
- COWERS
- CYNICAL
- DEPRAVED
- DOCILE
- ERRATIC
- EUPHEMISMS
- EXIGENCIES
- FLAIL
- FUGUES
- FUTILE
- HUNCHES
- IMPERCEPTIBLY
- IMPULSE
- INEVITABLE
- IRONIC
- ISOLATED
- LETHARGY
- MAROONED
- MASSIVE
- NAIVETE
- NUMB
- OBSTRUCTION
- ORNATELY
- PATHOLOGY
- PECULIAR
- PLATEAU
- PLATONIC
- POMPOUS
- PROGNOSIS
- QUEASY
- RECEDE
- SKEPTICAL
- STUPOR
- USURPED
- VAGUE
- VALID
- WARD

Flowers For Algernon Vocabulary Crossword 1

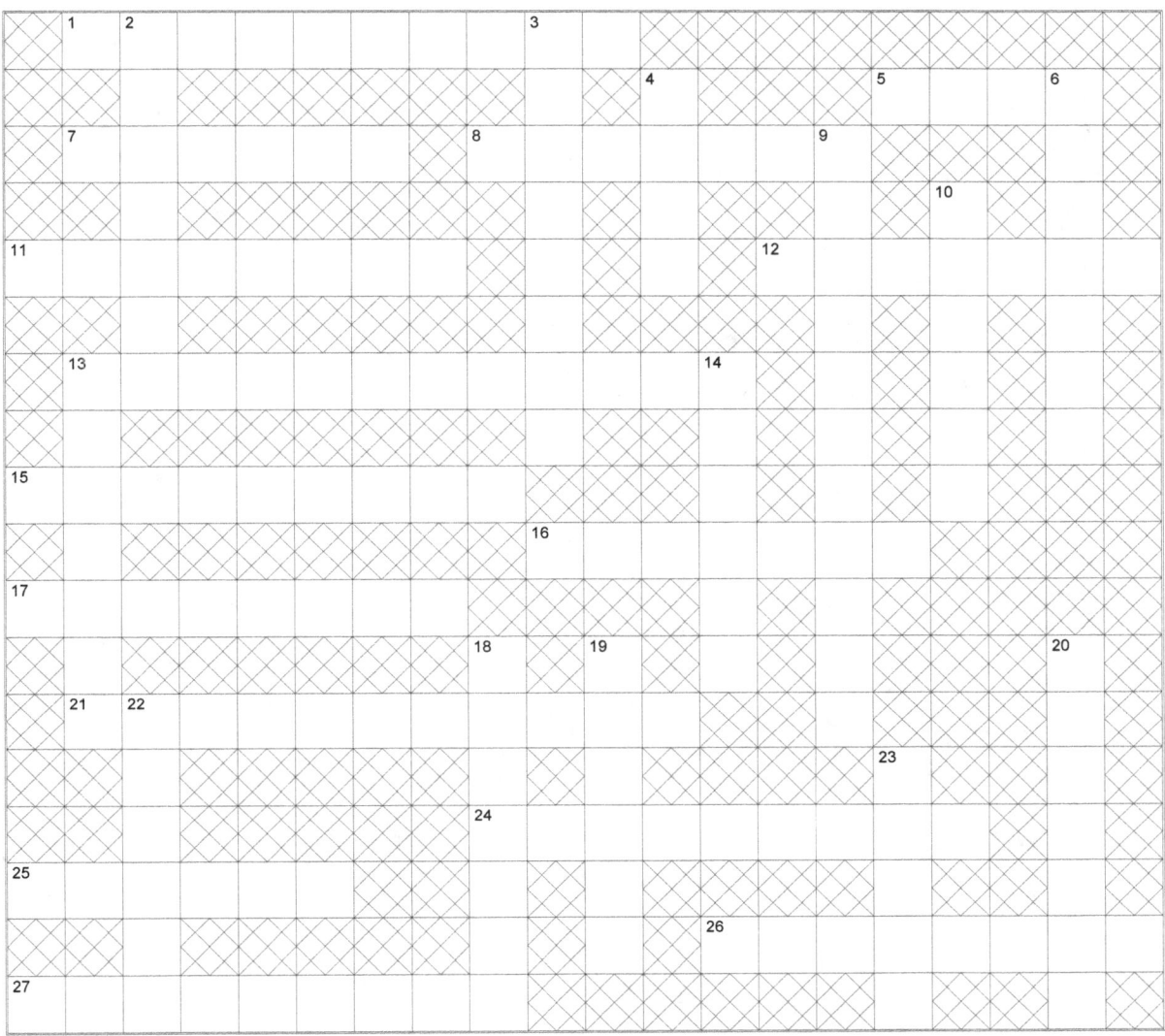

Across
1. Mild terms used for offensive ones
5. Unresponsive; unfeeling
7. Amnesiac conditions
8. Irregular; not uniform
11. Corrupt; wicked
12. Sudden wish or urge
13. Given out; dispensed
15. Knowing or sensing without rational processes
16. Expressing scorn and bitter mockery
17. Set apart or cut off from others
21. Gathered or piled up
24. Doubtful
25. Causing nausea; sickening
26. Unusual or eccentric; odd
27. Entrance hall

Down
2. Taken over or occupied without right
3. Abandoned or isolated with little hope of rescue
4. Try to prevent
6. Destructively or frenetically violent
9. Not easy to understand or analyze; complex
10. Having no useful result
13. Partial or total loss of memory
14. Yielding to supervision or management
18. Large
19. To move back or away from
20. Friendly
22. Cringes in fear
23. Indistinctly felt, perceived, or understood

Flowers For Algernon Vocabulary Crossword 1 Answer Key

Across
1. Mild terms used for offensive ones
5. Unresponsive; unfeeling
7. Amnesiac conditions
8. Irregular; not uniform
11. Corrupt; wicked
12. Sudden wish or urge
13. Given out; dispensed
15. Knowing or sensing without rational processes
16. Expressing scorn and bitter mockery
17. Set apart or cut off from others
21. Gathered or piled up
24. Doubtful
25. Causing nausea; sickening
26. Unusual or eccentric; odd
27. Entrance hall

Down
2. Taken over or occupied without right
3. Abandoned or isolated with little hope of rescue
4. Try to prevent
6. Destructively or frenetically violent
9. Not easy to understand or analyze; complex
10. Having no useful result
13. Partial or total loss of memory
14. Yielding to supervision or management
18. Large
19. To move back or away from
20. Friendly
22. Cringes in fear
23. Indistinctly felt, perceived, or understood

Flowers For Algernon Vocabulary Crossword 2

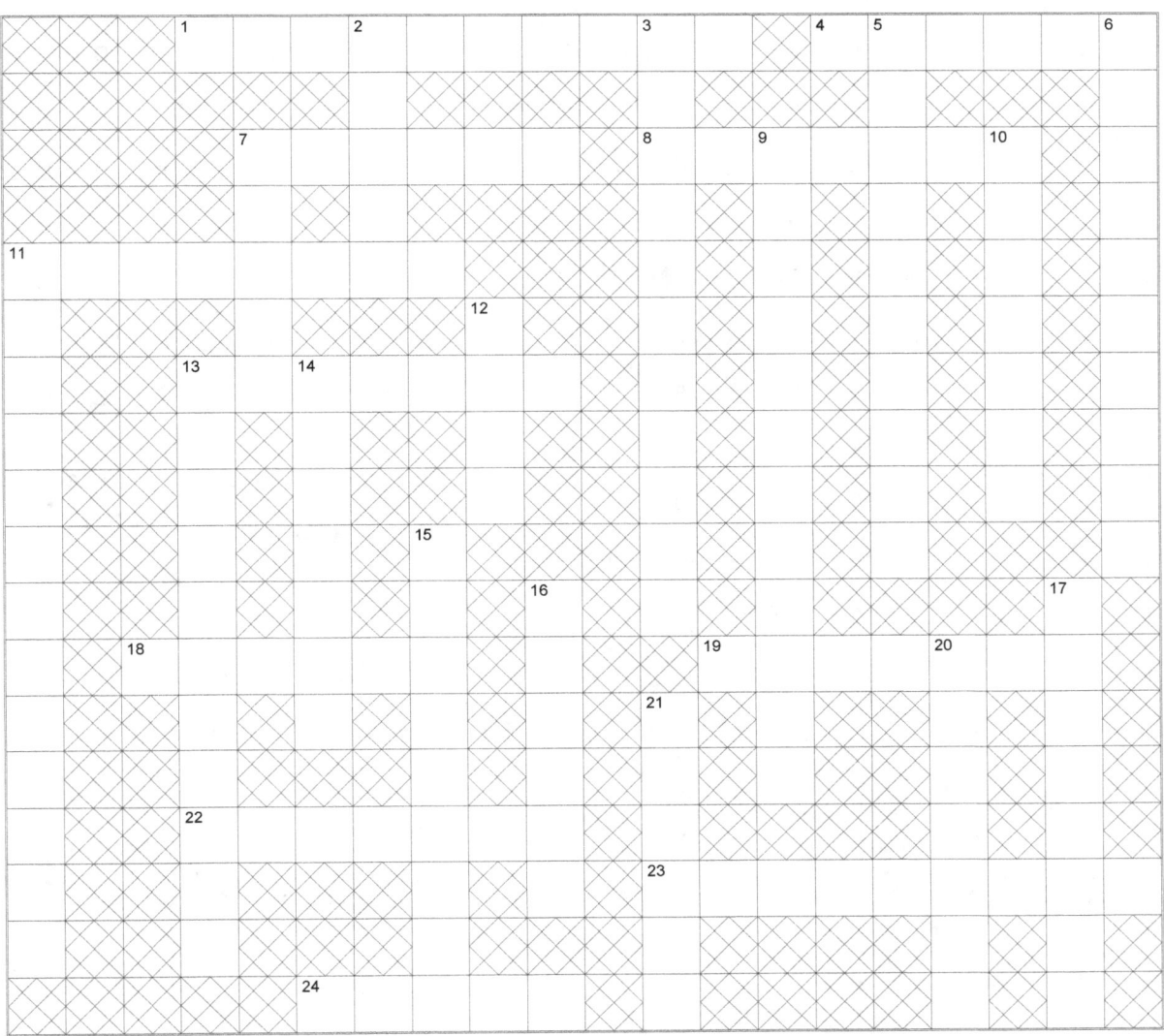

Across
1. Impossible to avoid or prevent
4. To move back or away from
7. Amnesiac conditions
8. Large
11. Corrupt; wicked
13. A stable or level state
18. Yielding to supervision or management
19. Taken over or occupied without right
22. Friendly
23. Prediction of the possible outcome of a disease
24. True; correct

Down
2. Indistinctly felt, perceived, or understood
3. Emitting light
5. Urgent requirements; pressing needs
6. Mild terms used for offensive ones
7. To strike or lash out violently
9. Placed on or over something else
10. Irregular; not uniform
11. A steady lowering of quality
12. Try to prevent
13. Seemingly contradictory but possibly true
14. Partial or total loss of memory
15. Doubtful
16. Having no useful result
17. To reprimand gently but earnestly
20. Arrogant; having excessive self-esteem
21. State of mental numbness

Flowers For Algernon Vocabulary Crossword 2 Answer Key

Across
1. Impossible to avoid or prevent
4. To move back or away from
7. Amnesiac conditions
8. Large
11. Corrupt; wicked
13. A stable or level state
18. Yielding to supervision or management
19. Taken over or occupied without right
22. Friendly
23. Prediction of the possible outcome of a disease
24. True; correct

Down
2. Indistinctly felt, perceived, or understood
3. Emitting light
5. Urgent requirements; pressing needs
6. Mild terms used for offensive ones
7. To strike or lash out violently
9. Placed on or over something else
10. Irregular; not uniform
11. A steady lowering of quality
12. Try to prevent
13. Seemingly contradictory but possibly true
14. Partial or total loss of memory
15. Doubtful
16. Having no useful result
17. To reprimand gently but earnestly
20. Arrogant; having excessive self-esteem
21. State of mental numbness

Flowers For Algernon Vocabulary Crossword 3

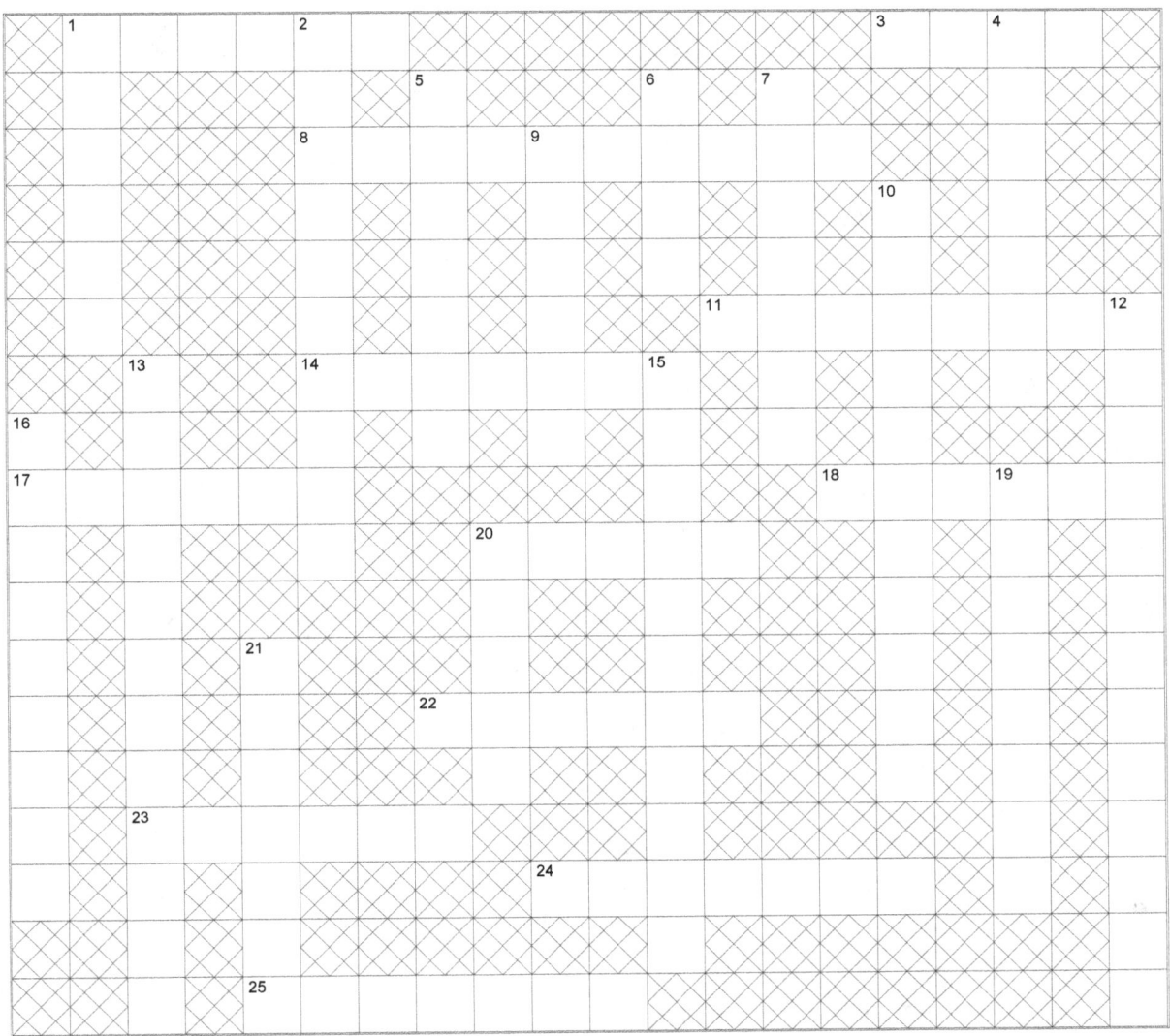

Across
1. Amnesiac conditions
3. Unresponsive; unfeeling
8. Impossible to avoid or prevent
11. Corrupt; wicked
14. Friendly
17. To move back or away from
18. Yielding to supervision or management
20. True; correct
22. Causing nausea; sickening
23. State of mental numbness
24. Assumes a crouched or cramped posture
25. Irregular; not uniform

Down
1. Having no useful result
2. Urgent requirements; pressing needs
4. Large
5. Destructively or frenetically violent
6. Try to prevent
7. A stable or level state
9. Contrary to what was expected or intended
10. Seemingly contradictory but possibly true
12. A steady lowering of quality
13. Surrounding
15. Emitting light
16. Prediction of the possible outcome of a disease
19. Set apart or cut off from others
20. Indistinctly felt, perceived, or understood
21. Sudden wish or urge

Flowers For Algernon Vocabulary Crossword 3 Answer Key

Across
1. Amnesiac conditions
3. Unresponsive; unfeeling
8. Impossible to avoid or prevent
11. Corrupt; wicked
14. Friendly
17. To move back or away from
18. Yielding to supervision or management
20. True; correct
22. Causing nausea; sickening
23. State of mental numbness
24. Assumes a crouched or cramped posture
25. Irregular; not uniform

Down
1. Having no useful result
2. Urgent requirements; pressing needs
4. Large
5. Destructively or frenetically violent
6. Try to prevent
7. A stable or level state
9. Contrary to what was expected or intended
10. Seemingly contradictory but possibly true
12. A steady lowering of quality
13. Surrounding
15. Emitting light
16. Prediction of the possible outcome of a disease
19. Set apart or cut off from others
20. Indistinctly felt, perceived, or understood
21. Sudden wish or urge

Flowers For Algernon Vocabulary Crossword 4

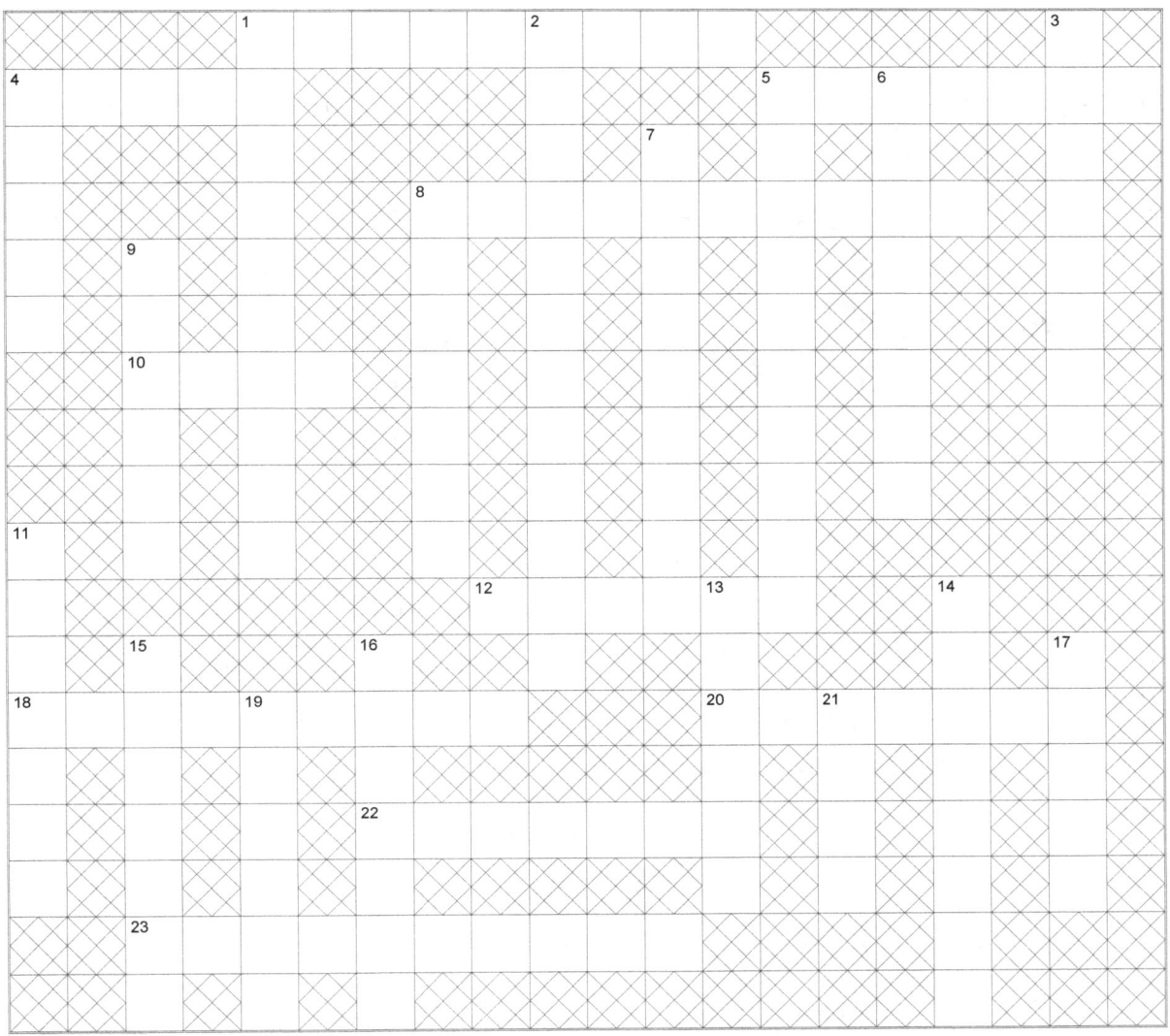

Across
1. Disliking intensely
4. Indistinctly felt, perceived, or understood
5. Sudden wish or urge
8. Extraordinary; outstanding
10. Try to prevent
12. To move back or away from
18. Entrance hall
20. Expressing scorn and bitter mockery
22. Friendly
23. Urgent requirements; pressing needs

Down
1. A depraved, corrupt, or vicious person
2. Placed on or over something else
3. Set apart or cut off from others
4. True; correct
5. Impossible to avoid or prevent
6. Spiritual or ideal, not physical
7. A calm state of mind
8. A stable or level state
9. Cringes in fear
11. The state of being unaware of something that most people know; innocence
13. Yielding to supervision or management
14. Unusual or eccentric; odd
15. Taken over or occupied without right
16. Assumes a crouched or cramped posture
17. To strike or lash out violently
19. Contrary to what was expected or intended
21. Unresponsive; unfeeling

Flowers For Algernon Vocabulary Crossword 4 Answer Key

			1 D	E	S	2 P	I	S	N	G			5	6			3 I	
4 V	A	G	U	E		U							I	M	P	U	L	S	E
A			G			P		7 C		N		L			O
L			E		8 P	H	E	N	O	M	E	N	A	L
I		9 C		N		L	R	M		V		T			A
D		O		E		A	I	P		I		O			T
		10 W	A	R	D	T	M	O		T		N			E
		E		A		E	M	S		A		I			D
		R		T		A	P	U		B		C
11 N		S		E		U	O	R		L
A					12 R	E	C	E	13 D	E		14 P
I		15 U		16 H		D			O			E	17 F
18 V	E	S	T	19 I	B	U	L	E		20 C	21 Y	N	I	C	A	L
E		U		R		N				I		U		U		A
T		R		O		22 C	O	R	D	I	A	L		I
E		P		N		H				E		M	B	I	L
		23 E	X	I	G	E	N	C	I	E	S			A
		D		C		S							R

Across
1. Disliking intensely
4. Indistinctly felt, perceived, or understood
5. Sudden wish or urge
8. Extraordinary; outstanding
10. Try to prevent
12. To move back or away from
18. Entrance hall
20. Expressing scorn and bitter mockery
22. Friendly
23. Urgent requirements; pressing needs

Down
1. A depraved, corrupt, or vicious person
2. Placed on or over something else
3. Set apart or cut off from others
4. True; correct
5. Impossible to avoid or prevent
6. Spiritual or ideal, not physical
7. A calm state of mind
8. A stable or level state
9. Cringes in fear
11. The state of being unaware of something that most people know; innocence
13. Yielding to supervision or management
14. Unusual or eccentric; odd
15. Taken over or occupied without right
16. Assumes a crouched or cramped posture
17. To strike or lash out violently
19. Contrary to what was expected or intended
21. Unresponsive; unfeeling

Flowers For Algernon Vocabulary Juggle Letters 1

1. ILOMITANPCI = 1. _____
   Something hinted or suggested

2. NISGOPSRO = 2. _____
   Prediction of the possible outcome of a disease

3. IGNCSXEEEI = 3. _____
   Urgent requirements; pressing needs

4. AYHLNRTIB = 4. _____
   A maze

5. KELTISAPC = 5. _____
   Doubtful

6. SREERBK = 6. _____
   Destructively or frenetically violent

7. VDPEDERA = 7. _____
   Corrupt; wicked

8. IPRAECUL = 8. _____
   Unusual or eccentric; odd

9. RORDPEUEC = 9. _____
   Series of steps to accomplish something

10. ASNPMICNOGES = 10. _____
    Surrounding

11. WRAD = 11. _____
    Try to prevent

12. AIDVL = 12. _____
    True; correct

13. AAXPACORDLI = 13. _____
    Seemingly contradictory but possibly true

14. LUEVETBIS = 14. _____
    Entrance hall

15. VIEATNE = 15. _____
    The state of being unaware of something that most people know; innocence

Flowers For Algernon Vocabulary Juggle Letters 1 Answer Key

1. ILOMITANPCI = 1. IMPLICATION
Something hinted or suggested

2. NISGOPSRO = 2. PROGNOSIS
Prediction of the possible outcome of a disease

3. IGNCSXEEEI = 3. EXIGENCIES
Urgent requirements; pressing needs

4. AYHLNRTIB = 4. LABYRINTH
A maze

5. KELTISAPC = 5. SKEPTICAL
Doubtful

6. SREERBK = 6. BERSERK
Destructively or frenetically violent

7. VDPEDERA = 7. DEPRAVED
Corrupt; wicked

8. IPRAECUL = 8. PECULIAR
Unusual or eccentric; odd

9. RORDPEUEC = 9. PROCEDURE
Series of steps to accomplish something

10. ASNPMICNOGES = 10. ENCOMPASSING
Surrounding

11. WRAD = 11. WARD
Try to prevent

12. AIDVL = 12. VALID
True; correct

13. AAXPACORDLI = 13. PARADOXICAL
Seemingly contradictory but possibly true

14. LUEVETBIS = 14. VESTIBULE
Entrance hall

15. VIEATNE = 15. NAIVETE
The state of being unaware of something that most people know; innocence

Flowers For Algernon Vocabulary Juggle Letters 2

1. AIDOLCR = 1. _____
Friendly

2. NSPSIEDGI = 2. _____
Disliking intensely

3. DREECE = 3. _____
To move back or away from

4. UYESAQ = 4. _____
Causing nausea; sickening

5. EASSVIM = 5. _____
Large

6. UITAIPSNJXTOO = 6. _____
Placement side by side for comparison

7. UCEDROERP = 7. _____
Series of steps to accomplish something

8. ITSGOAOLIBN = 8. _____
Duties or promises

9. RIBNHLAYT = 9. _____
A maze

10. ONLICAPT =10. _____
Spiritual or ideal, not physical

11. RAERCTI =11. _____
Irregular; not uniform

12. LOCDTCPEIMA =12. _____
Not easy to understand or analyze; complex

13. CILKPESTA =13. _____
Doubtful

14. ONRDEIRTITAEO =14. _____
A steady lowering of quality

15. OMNRDAOE =15. _____
Abandoned or isolated with little hope of rescue

Flowers For Algernon Vocabulary Juggle Letters 2 Answer Key

1. AIDOLCR = 1. CORDIAL
Friendly

2. NSPSIEDGI = 2. DESPISING
Disliking intensely

3. DREECE = 3. RECEDE
To move back or away from

4. UYESAQ = 4. QUEASY
Causing nausea; sickening

5. EASSVIM = 5. MASSIVE
Large

6. UITAIPSNJXTOO = 6. JUXTAPOSITION
Placement side by side for comparison

7. UCEDROERP = 7. PROCEDURE
Series of steps to accomplish something

8. ITSGOAOLIBN = 8. OBLIGATIONS
Duties or promises

9. RIBNHLAYT = 9. LABYRINTH
A maze

10. ONLICAPT = 10. PLATONIC
Spiritual or ideal, not physical

11. RAERCTI = 11. ERRATIC
Irregular; not uniform

12. LOCDTCPEIMA = 12. COMPLICATED
Not easy to understand or analyze; complex

13. CILKPESTA = 13. SKEPTICAL
Doubtful

14. ONRDEIRTITAEO = 14. DETERIORATION
A steady lowering of quality

15. OMNRDAOE = 15. MAROONED
Abandoned or isolated with little hope of rescue

Flowers For Algernon Vocabulary Juggle Letters 3

1. LAUPCIER = 1. _____
   Unusual or eccentric; odd

2. LMSCIEENTNU = 2. _____
   Emitting light

3. LAAEPTU = 3. _____
   A stable or level state

4. YGPOOTHLA = 4. _____
   The scientific study of disease

5. ONAROEMD = 5. _____
   Abandoned or isolated with little hope of rescue

6. LBHTNIRAY = 6. _____
   A maze

7. SHHUECN = 7. _____
   Assumes a crouched or cramped posture

8. IEATVIELBN = 8. _____
   Impossible to avoid or prevent

9. ACAXOLPIRDA = 9. _____
   Seemingly contradictory but possibly true

10. EAVENIT =10. _____
    The state of being unaware of something that most people know; innocence

11. SIICXEEEGN =11. _____
    Urgent requirements; pressing needs

12. IRNCOI =12. _____
    Contrary to what was expected or intended

13. IATNCPOL =13. _____
    Spiritual or ideal, not physical

14. PGDSIENIS =14. _____
    Disliking intensely

15. SIEETVULB =15. _____
    Entrance hall

Flowers For Algernon Vocabulary Juggle Letters 3 Answer Key

1. LAUPCIER = 1. PECULIAR
Unusual or eccentric; odd

2. LMSCIEENTNU = 2. LUMINESCENT
Emitting light

3. LAAEPTU = 3. PLATEAU
A stable or level state

4. YGPOOTHLA = 4. PATHOLOGY
The scientific study of disease

5. ONAROEMD = 5. MAROONED
Abandoned or isolated with little hope of rescue

6. LBHTNIRAY = 6. LABYRINTH
A maze

7. SHHUECN = 7. HUNCHES
Assumes a crouched or cramped posture

8. IEATVIELBN = 8. INEVITABLE
Impossible to avoid or prevent

9. ACAXOLPIRDA = 9. PARADOXICAL
Seemingly contradictory but possibly true

10. EAVENIT =10. NAIVETE
The state of being unaware of something that most people know; innocence

11. SIICXEEEGN =11. EXIGENCIES
Urgent requirements; pressing needs

12. IRNCOI =12. IRONIC
Contrary to what was expected or intended

13. IATNCPOL =13. PLATONIC
Spiritual or ideal, not physical

14. PGDSIENIS =14. DESPISING
Disliking intensely

15. SIEETVULB =15. VESTIBULE
Entrance hall

Flowers For Algernon Vocabulary Juggle Letters 4

1. TEIBILNAVE = 1. _____
   Impossible to avoid or prevent

2. OATLGSNBIOI = 2. _____
   Duties or promises

3. OLMNEHPEAN = 3. _____
   Extraordinary; outstanding

4. AEPEVDDR = 4. _____
   Corrupt; wicked

5. UBNM = 5. _____
   Unresponsive; unfeeling

6. ENVATEI = 6. _____
   The state of being unaware of something that most people know; innocence

7. RTRIACE = 7. _____
   Irregular; not uniform

8. PELAIRCU = 8. _____
   Unusual or eccentric; odd

9. OATNLIPC = 9. _____
   Spiritual or ideal, not physical

10. SERWOC = 10. _____
    Cringes in fear

11. EORUPRECD = 11. _____
    Series of steps to accomplish something

12. SLIUEBETV = 12. _____
    Entrance hall

13. POUPSOM = 13. _____
    Arrogant; having excessive self-esteem

14. CMTEAUCUADL = 14. _____
    Gathered or piled up

15. OINIARDTTEROE = 15. _____
    A steady lowering of quality

Flowers For Algernon Vocabulary Juggle Letters 4 Answer Key

1. TEIBILNAVE = 1. INEVITABLE
   Impossible to avoid or prevent

2. OATLGSNBIOI = 2. OBLIGATIONS
   Duties or promises

3. OLMNEHPEAN = 3. PHENOMENAL
   Extraordinary; outstanding

4. AEPEVDDR = 4. DEPRAVED
   Corrupt; wicked

5. UBNM = 5. NUMB
   Unresponsive; unfeeling

6. ENVATEI = 6. NAIVETE
   The state of being unaware of something that most people know; innocence

7. RTRIACE = 7. ERRATIC
   Irregular; not uniform

8. PELAIRCU = 8. PECULIAR
   Unusual or eccentric; odd

9. OATNLIPC = 9. PLATONIC
   Spiritual or ideal, not physical

10. SERWOC = 10. COWERS
    Cringes in fear

11. EORUPRECD = 11. PROCEDURE
    Series of steps to accomplish something

12. SLIUEBETV = 12. VESTIBULE
    Entrance hall

13. POUPSOM = 13. POMPOUS
    Arrogant; having excessive self-esteem

14. CMTEAUCUADL = 14. ACCUMULATED
    Gathered or piled up

15. OINIARDTTEROE = 15. DETERIORATION
    A steady lowering of quality

PHENOMENAL	Extraordinary; outstanding
POMPOUS	Arrogant; having excessive self-esteem
NAIVETE	The state of being unaware of something that most people know; innocence
SUPERIMPOSED	Placed on or over something else
VALID	True; correct
ERRATIC	Irregular; not uniform
EUPHEMISMS	Mild terms used for offensive ones

INEVITABLE	Impossible to avoid or prevent
FUTILE	Having no useful result
ACCUMULATED	Gathered or piled up
JUXTAPOSITION	Placement side by side for comparison
USURPED	Taken over or occupied without right
PATHOLOGY	The scientific study of disease
PERMANENT	Unchanging

BERSERK	Destructively or frenetically violent
APPRENTICE	One who is learning a trade or occupation
IMPLICATION	Something hinted or suggested
DESPISING	Disliking intensely
PROCEDURE	Series of steps to accomplish something
IRONIC	Contrary to what was expected or intended
WARD	Try to prevent

PECULIAR	Unusual or eccentric; odd
CORDIAL	Friendly
DEGENERATE	A depraved, corrupt, or vicious person
DETERIORATION	A steady lowering of quality
ORNATELY	Flashy, showy, intricate in style or manner
PARADOXICAL	Seemingly contradictory but possibly true
ISOLATED	Set apart or cut off from others

SKEPTICAL	Doubtful
EXIGENCIES	Urgent requirements; pressing needs
VESTIBULE	Entrance hall
PROGNOSIS	Prediction of the possible outcome of a disease
LUMINESCENT	Emitting light
AMNESIA	Partial or total loss of memory
NUMB	Unresponsive; unfeeling

MAROONED	Abandoned or isolated with little hope of rescue
PRECAUTION	Action taken to prevent possible danger
RECEDE	To move back or away from
PLATEAU	A stable or level state
QUEASY	Causing nausea; sickening
OBSTRUCTION	Something in the way
STUPOR	State of mental numbness

FUGUES	Amnesiac conditions
CYNICAL	Expressing scorn and bitter mockery
CONSISTENT	Reliable or uniform
OBLIGATIONS	Duties or promises
DEPRAVED	Corrupt; wicked
CONSCIOUS	Aware
PLATONIC	Spiritual or ideal, not physical

FLAIL	To strike or lash out violently
LETHARGY	State of sluggishness or inactivity
IMPERCEPTIBLY	Without being seen or noticed
INTUITION	Knowing or sensing without rational processes
IMPULSE	Sudden wish or urge
ENCOMPASSING	Surrounding
VAGUE	Indistinctly felt, perceived, or understood

LABYRINTH	A maze
DOCILE	Yielding to supervision or management
COMPOSURE	A calm state of mind
COMPLICATED	Not easy to understand or analyze; complex
MASSIVE	Large
ADMONISH	To reprimand gently but earnestly
COWERS	Cringes in fear

ADMINISTERED	Given out; dispensed
HUNCHES	Assumes a crouched or cramped posture

Flowers For Algernon

MAROONED	POMPOUS	WARD	DETERIORATION	PLATONIC
ORNATELY	VESTIBULE	APPRENTICE	VAGUE	COMPLICATED
EUPHEMISMS	LABYRINTH	FREE SPACE	SUPERIMPOSED	CONSCIOUS
IRONIC	CORDIAL	RECEDE	PRECAUTION	OBSTRUCTION
PHENOMENAL	COWERS	NAIVETE	INEVITABLE	USURPED

Flowers For Algernon

SKEPTICAL	EXIGENCIES	VALID	DEGENERATE	BERSERK
CYNICAL	FUTILE	PROCEDURE	STUPOR	ISOLATED
COMPOSURE	PECULIAR	FREE SPACE	LUMINESCENT	ADMONISH
AMNESIA	CONSISTENT	HUNCHES	ACCUMULATED	ENCOMPASSING
PATHOLOGY	PLATEAU	ERRATIC	FUGUES	ADMINISTERED

Flowers For Algernon

PROGNOSIS	ORNATELY	PERMANENT	POMPOUS	INTUITION
OBLIGATIONS	INEVITABLE	ADMINISTERED	ERRATIC	VAGUE
ADMONISH	COMPOSURE	FREE SPACE	COMPLICATED	PARADOXICAL
OBSTRUCTION	NAIVETE	DEPRAVED	ISOLATED	IRONIC
COWERS	USURPED	FUTILE	ENCOMPASSING	PROCEDURE

Flowers For Algernon

VALID	CONSCIOUS	ACCUMULATED	IMPULSE	LUMINESCENT
PHENOMENAL	CYNICAL	DETERIORATION	IMPLICATION	PECULIAR
BERSERK	DEGENERATE	FREE SPACE	QUEASY	PATHOLOGY
VESTIBULE	PLATEAU	CORDIAL	STUPOR	DOCILE
DESPISING	HUNCHES	SUPERIMPOSED	EXIGENCIES	EUPHEMISMS

Flowers For Algernon

PRECAUTION	COMPOSURE	FLAIL	MAROONED	DESPISING
ADMINISTERED	DOCILE	ENCOMPASSING	RECEDE	SKEPTICAL
FUTILE	EUPHEMISMS	FREE SPACE	ACCUMULATED	INEVITABLE
INTUITION	USURPED	SUPERIMPOSED	ERRATIC	FUGUES
JUXTAPOSITION	STUPOR	IMPERCEPTIBLY	PLATEAU	ADMONISH

Flowers For Algernon

LABYRINTH	PERMANENT	PHENOMENAL	QUEASY	LUMINESCENT
CONSCIOUS	COMPLICATED	PATHOLOGY	ISOLATED	PROGNOSIS
VESTIBULE	WARD	FREE SPACE	MASSIVE	POMPOUS
CYNICAL	IMPLICATION	DEGENERATE	NUMB	AMNESIA
HUNCHES	VALID	LETHARGY	IRONIC	EXIGENCIES

Flowers For Algernon

ADMINISTERED	CYNICAL	SKEPTICAL	OBLIGATIONS	VAGUE
IMPLICATION	EXIGENCIES	LETHARGY	ENCOMPASSING	LUMINESCENT
PHENOMENAL	DEGENERATE	FREE SPACE	PRECAUTION	ORNATELY
DESPISING	AMNESIA	DETERIORATION	ACCUMULATED	PLATONIC
JUXTAPOSITION	COMPOSURE	VESTIBULE	PECULIAR	STUPOR

Flowers For Algernon

WARD	PROCEDURE	CONSCIOUS	INEVITABLE	PARADOXICAL
LABYRINTH	USURPED	ERRATIC	PERMANENT	FUTILE
CORDIAL	EUPHEMISMS	FREE SPACE	MAROONED	SUPERIMPOSED
DOCILE	DEPRAVED	OBSTRUCTION	FLAIL	IMPERCEPTIBLY
VALID	NUMB	IRONIC	PATHOLOGY	BERSERK

Flowers For Algernon

OBSTRUCTION	ENCOMPASSING	FUTILE	PERMANENT	VALID
OBLIGATIONS	USURPED	FLAIL	DESPISING	PRECAUTION
DEGENERATE	JUXTAPOSITION	FREE SPACE	LUMINESCENT	CYNICAL
SKEPTICAL	SUPERIMPOSED	ORNATELY	IMPULSE	ISOLATED
QUEASY	PLATEAU	MAROONED	ADMINISTERED	NAIVETE

Flowers For Algernon

PROGNOSIS	EUPHEMISMS	PROCEDURE	HUNCHES	COMPOSURE
VESTIBULE	PATHOLOGY	DOCILE	PARADOXICAL	CORDIAL
PLATONIC	DETERIORATION	FREE SPACE	COWERS	ERRATIC
RECEDE	LETHARGY	VAGUE	PHENOMENAL	FUGUES
IRONIC	APPRENTICE	ADMONISH	STUPOR	COMPLICATED

Flowers For Algernon

POMPOUS	APPRENTICE	MAROONED	INEVITABLE	FUTILE
RECEDE	SUPERIMPOSED	CONSCIOUS	BERSERK	PLATEAU
EXIGENCIES	NAIVETE	FREE SPACE	LUMINESCENT	DEPRAVED
PROCEDURE	IMPULSE	USURPED	PRECAUTION	OBLIGATIONS
PLATONIC	PHENOMENAL	SKEPTICAL	LABYRINTH	CORDIAL

Flowers For Algernon

JUXTAPOSITION	VAGUE	CYNICAL	CONSISTENT	FLAIL
ORNATELY	IRONIC	EUPHEMISMS	VESTIBULE	MASSIVE
ACCUMULATED	FUGUES	FREE SPACE	WARD	DEGENERATE
HUNCHES	DESPISING	AMNESIA	COWERS	PERMANENT
DOCILE	DETERIORATION	VALID	PECULIAR	INTUITION

Flowers For Algernon

VAGUE	DETERIORATION	VESTIBULE	COWERS	MASSIVE
IMPLICATION	ERRATIC	INEVITABLE	IMPERCEPTIBLY	LUMINESCENT
PECULIAR	CONSCIOUS	FREE SPACE	DEGENERATE	FLAIL
PRECAUTION	ACCUMULATED	PARADOXICAL	ADMONISH	NUMB
DEPRAVED	IMPULSE	IRONIC	OBSTRUCTION	ENCOMPASSING

Flowers For Algernon

FUGUES	AMNESIA	CONSISTENT	COMPLICATED	PATHOLOGY
LETHARGY	ADMINISTERED	LABYRINTH	CORDIAL	EXIGENCIES
SUPERIMPOSED	HUNCHES	FREE SPACE	PLATONIC	WARD
PERMANENT	PHENOMENAL	JUXTAPOSITION	PROCEDURE	SKEPTICAL
EUPHEMISMS	DOCILE	PLATEAU	DESPISING	NAIVETE

Flowers For Algernon

PROCEDURE	IMPULSE	PARADOXICAL	CYNICAL	IRONIC
DEGENERATE	OBSTRUCTION	COMPLICATED	PRECAUTION	FLAIL
PERMANENT	ENCOMPASSING	FREE SPACE	ERRATIC	EUPHEMISMS
COWERS	COMPOSURE	ADMONISH	DEPRAVED	EXIGENCIES
LABYRINTH	INTUITION	FUGUES	CORDIAL	PROGNOSIS

Flowers For Algernon

NAIVETE	SUPERIMPOSED	VAGUE	VESTIBULE	OBLIGATIONS
ACCUMULATED	ORNATELY	STUPOR	RECEDE	NUMB
ISOLATED	CONSISTENT	FREE SPACE	APPRENTICE	QUEASY
HUNCHES	WARD	VALID	PATHOLOGY	MAROONED
SKEPTICAL	DOCILE	ADMINISTERED	BERSERK	PLATEAU

Flowers For Algernon

WARD	NUMB	APPRENTICE	PHENOMENAL	STUPOR
SUPERIMPOSED	FUGUES	INTUITION	INEVITABLE	PROGNOSIS
OBSTRUCTION	CONSCIOUS	FREE SPACE	CONSISTENT	MAROONED
AMNESIA	ACCUMULATED	SKEPTICAL	PROCEDURE	DETERIORATION
RECEDE	IMPERCEPTIBLY	HUNCHES	CORDIAL	MASSIVE

Flowers For Algernon

ENCOMPASSING	OBLIGATIONS	LETHARGY	POMPOUS	USURPED
NAIVETE	LUMINESCENT	IMPLICATION	BERSERK	PLATEAU
ISOLATED	ERRATIC	FREE SPACE	VESTIBULE	VALID
EUPHEMISMS	PATHOLOGY	LABYRINTH	PERMANENT	DEGENERATE
EXIGENCIES	DESPISING	PLATONIC	COMPOSURE	QUEASY

Flowers For Algernon

OBLIGATIONS	ERRATIC	DESPISING	DOCILE	HUNCHES
SUPERIMPOSED	VAGUE	ADMONISH	EUPHEMISMS	DETERIORATION
COMPOSURE	ISOLATED	FREE SPACE	QUEASY	EXIGENCIES
LABYRINTH	MAROONED	PERMANENT	PARADOXICAL	ADMINISTERED
PRECAUTION	INEVITABLE	CYNICAL	BERSERK	APPRENTICE

Flowers For Algernon

NUMB	IRONIC	SKEPTICAL	PATHOLOGY	PLATEAU
JUXTAPOSITION	PROCEDURE	IMPULSE	NAIVETE	CONSISTENT
COWERS	PECULIAR	FREE SPACE	LETHARGY	VESTIBULE
OBSTRUCTION	IMPERCEPTIBLY	VALID	RECEDE	ENCOMPASSING
COMPLICATED	USURPED	CONSCIOUS	PROGNOSIS	DEPRAVED

Flowers For Algernon

SUPERIMPOSED	IMPULSE	MAROONED	NAIVETE	WARD
PROCEDURE	LETHARGY	PECULIAR	ADMINISTERED	ADMONISH
LABYRINTH	DEPRAVED	FREE SPACE	COMPLICATED	STUPOR
IMPLICATION	HUNCHES	JUXTAPOSITION	EUPHEMISMS	MASSIVE
ORNATELY	FLAIL	SKEPTICAL	ERRATIC	PLATONIC

Flowers For Algernon

COMPOSURE	DESPISING	IMPERCEPTIBLY	INTUITION	USURPED
BERSERK	CONSISTENT	QUEASY	PARADOXICAL	ENCOMPASSING
VESTIBULE	EXIGENCIES	FREE SPACE	DOCILE	FUTILE
VAGUE	DEGENERATE	NUMB	APPRENTICE	IRONIC
OBSTRUCTION	PERMANENT	COWERS	OBLIGATIONS	ISOLATED

Flowers For Algernon

PHENOMENAL	OBSTRUCTION	RECEDE	BERSERK	ORNATELY
INEVITABLE	DEGENERATE	LABYRINTH	MAROONED	PLATEAU
LUMINESCENT	EUPHEMISMS	FREE SPACE	LETHARGY	EXIGENCIES
PROCEDURE	PARADOXICAL	COMPLICATED	POMPOUS	PLATONIC
QUEASY	ACCUMULATED	NAIVETE	PRECAUTION	CONSCIOUS

Flowers For Algernon

DESPISING	FUGUES	ERRATIC	ADMINISTERED	COWERS
VESTIBULE	IRONIC	CYNICAL	WARD	JUXTAPOSITION
ADMONISH	DOCILE	FREE SPACE	ISOLATED	VALID
AMNESIA	MASSIVE	USURPED	IMPERCEPTIBLY	IMPLICATION
VAGUE	OBLIGATIONS	FLAIL	PERMANENT	COMPOSURE

Flowers For Algernon

OBSTRUCTION	SKEPTICAL	LETHARGY	PROCEDURE	ADMINISTERED
IMPULSE	COWERS	QUEASY	IMPLICATION	PLATEAU
CYNICAL	JUXTAPOSITION	FREE SPACE	DEGENERATE	DOCILE
CORDIAL	STUPOR	HUNCHES	DEPRAVED	DETERIORATION
APPRENTICE	INTUITION	CONSCIOUS	FLAIL	COMPLICATED

Flowers For Algernon

ENCOMPASSING	POMPOUS	EUPHEMISMS	OBLIGATIONS	ACCUMULATED
ISOLATED	SUPERIMPOSED	VAGUE	INEVITABLE	NUMB
VESTIBULE	COMPOSURE	FREE SPACE	PHENOMENAL	DESPISING
USURPED	ORNATELY	MASSIVE	PLATONIC	FUGUES
AMNESIA	LUMINESCENT	LABYRINTH	MAROONED	PECULIAR

Flowers For Algernon

AMNESIA	PROGNOSIS	PRECAUTION	EUPHEMISMS	FUTILE
COMPOSURE	FLAIL	INTUITION	PARADOXICAL	PLATEAU
IRONIC	ISOLATED	FREE SPACE	QUEASY	HUNCHES
PATHOLOGY	NAIVETE	CONSISTENT	BERSERK	PLATONIC
RECEDE	VALID	OBSTRUCTION	POMPOUS	NUMB

Flowers For Algernon

PROCEDURE	DETERIORATION	MASSIVE	USURPED	SKEPTICAL
CYNICAL	CONSCIOUS	APPRENTICE	COWERS	PERMANENT
ERRATIC	COMPLICATED	FREE SPACE	VAGUE	SUPERIMPOSED
JUXTAPOSITION	LUMINESCENT	ADMONISH	PHENOMENAL	IMPULSE
EXIGENCIES	DESPISING	DEGENERATE	IMPLICATION	ADMINISTERED

Flowers For Algernon

COMPLICATED	DETERIORATION	ADMINISTERED	DEGENERATE	STUPOR
FUGUES	FUTILE	NUMB	COMPOSURE	ORNATELY
LUMINESCENT	PATHOLOGY	FREE SPACE	ACCUMULATED	PERMANENT
VAGUE	LABYRINTH	AMNESIA	PROGNOSIS	ENCOMPASSING
IMPLICATION	SKEPTICAL	POMPOUS	ADMONISH	DEPRAVED

Flowers For Algernon

DESPISING	SUPERIMPOSED	VESTIBULE	PROCEDURE	MAROONED
NAIVETE	VALID	PLATEAU	PRECAUTION	BERSERK
JUXTAPOSITION	PECULIAR	FREE SPACE	ISOLATED	CONSCIOUS
IRONIC	INTUITION	WARD	IMPERCEPTIBLY	PHENOMENAL
DOCILE	COWERS	RECEDE	CYNICAL	MASSIVE

Flowers For Algernon

NUMB	ISOLATED	PATHOLOGY	VAGUE	ENCOMPASSING
INTUITION	PERMANENT	FUTILE	MAROONED	BERSERK
WARD	PLATEAU	FREE SPACE	EUPHEMISMS	EXIGENCIES
INEVITABLE	ORNATELY	APPRENTICE	STUPOR	COMPLICATED
VALID	HUNCHES	PROCEDURE	PRECAUTION	ADMONISH

Flowers For Algernon

OBSTRUCTION	NAIVETE	USURPED	ADMINISTERED	PARADOXICAL
AMNESIA	DETERIORATION	CYNICAL	VESTIBULE	CONSISTENT
QUEASY	JUXTAPOSITION	FREE SPACE	MASSIVE	SUPERIMPOSED
COWERS	CONSCIOUS	DOCILE	ERRATIC	LETHARGY
IRONIC	PECULIAR	DESPISING	RECEDE	SKEPTICAL